GREAT WORLD WAR II WEAPONS

THE MP40 "SCHMEISSER"

Other titles in this series:

The Bismarck
by Robert Jackson

Tiger Tank
by Roger Ford

Panther Tank
by Matthew Hughes and Chris Mann

B-17 Flying Fortress
by Robert Jackson

GREAT WORLD WAR II WEAPONS

THE MP40 “SCHMEISSER”

MIKE INGRAM

amber
BOOKS

This Amber edition published in 2018
First published in 2001

Published by
Amber Books Ltd
United House
North Road
London N7 NDP
United Kingdom
www.amberbooks.co.uk
Instagram: www.instagram.com/amberbooksltd
Facebook: www.facebook.com/amberbooks
Twitter: @amberbooks

ISBN: 978-1-78274-683-6

Printed in the United States

Picture credits
Bundesarchiv: 39, 53
Ian Post: 29, 40, 49, 55, 56, 57
Novosti: 69
Robert Hunt Library: 60
TRH Pictures: 2–3, 6–7, 8, 9 (IWM), 10 (IWM), 11 (IWM), 12 (IWM), 13, 14, 15 (IWM), 16 (b), 18 (IWM), 19 (IWM), 20–21, 22, 24–25, 26–27 (ESP), 28, 30, 31, 32–33, 34, 35, 36–37, 38, 41, 42–43 (Bundesarchiv), 44, 45, 48, 50 (Bundesarchiv), 51, 52, 54, 58–59, 61, 62–63, 64 (IWM), 65 (Bundesarchiv), 66, 68, 70–71, 73, 74, 75, 76–77, 78 (G D Taylor), 79 (IWM), 80 (US National Archives), 80–81, 82, 84–85 (IWM), 85 (b) (US National Archives), 86, 87, 89 (IWM), 90

Artwork credits
Aerospace: 70, 90
De Agostini: 16–17, 23, 72, 82–83, 88–89
Guy Smith (Mainline Design): 46–47

CONTENTS

CHAPTER 1

Genesis of the Machine Pistol

Trench warfare in World War I taught the need for a weapon that could easily be carried and fired by one man yet deliver a devastating hail of bullets. The genesis of the machine pistol, however, can be traced back even further, to the automatic pistols of the 1890s.

At this time the major arms manufacturers, such as Colt, Steyr and FN, were all racing to develop a pistol that did not need cocking every time it was fired. It was an American, Hugo Borchardt, who produced the first workable design incorporating a removable box magazine. When his employer, the Winchester Arms Company in Connecticut, showed no interest in his design, he approached Ludwig Löewe & Co in Berlin (which would later form the nucleus of the Deutsche Waffen und Munitionsfabriken - DWM). Borchardt was offered a position with the company and his pistol was put into production in 1893. The significant features of the gun included a spring-operated box magazine in the grip that fed into a toggle-locked bolt, as well as a provision for a detachable rifle-type stock. Borchardt also worked on the design of the C96 Mauser pistol, which used many of his innovations.

Another member of Borchardt's design team was Georg Luger, who would go on to develop Borchardt's design into probably one of the best-known pistols in the world. Luger used the recoil movement of the gun to open the toggle lock and to move the pivot above the bore. This allowed the breech block to move to the back of the receiver and compress the return spring. The spring then forced the breech block back into place behind the barrel. This in turn returned the toggle joint and receiver back to the firing position ready to fire the bottlenecked 7.65mm (0.301in) Mauser cartridge. The Parabellum Pistolle Modell 1900, as it was called, was criticised for its lack of stopping power and the lightness of the round.

The biggest problem that all the designers had was the shape of the cartridge. The rim, which was used to seat the

Left: A German machine gun section advancing during the Battle of Aisne in 1918. Machine guns gave infantry extra firepower, but moving them was a major ordeal due to their size and weight.

round and control the head space, made it almost impossible to feed rounds from a box magazine. Rifle manufacturers had encountered the same problem when incorporating box magazines into their manually-operated repeating rifles in the 1880s. In August 1887 a Swiss, Major Rubin, introduced a rimless brass case at a comparison test in the Confederation Military Gunnery School at Wallenstadt. This new cartridge had a groove, or cannelure, that allowed the extractor to grip the casing, while seating and headspace were achieved by the overall profile and the thickness of the projectile's cartridge case. The Bavarian military representative, von Xylander, reported to Munich that the superiority of the Rubin cartridge had been clearly proved. It was not long after that other pistol manufacturers began to include this revolutionary development in their own designs.

GERMAN EXPERIMENTATION

At the end of the 1870s, the German Rifle Testing Commission had been experimenting with new military cartridges, with the purpose of saving weight without any degradation of performance, so that soldiers could carry more ammunition without increasing the load they already carried. To begin with, efforts concentrated on the reduction of the 11mm (0.43in) calibre of the ammunition that was in use at the time. With hard lead (93 per cent lead, 7 per cent tin) bullets, tests found that 9mm (0.354in) was the smallest calibre at which black-powder shooting under military conditions would be successful. However, a build-up of deposits of lead in the barrel quickly made the weapon unusable. Further tests were carried out with copper and brass bullets. Although they performed well in the barrel, because of the lightness of the material they lost speed and energy too quickly. The Rifle Testing Commission went back to the jacketed bullet whose invention is attributed to the Prussian Major Bode. Its design consisted of a lead core with a jacket of copper, brass, steel or nickel that could not be worn away by rifling grooves. Further tests at Spandau found the best jacket to be copper/nickel-plated sheet steel with a core of 95 per cent lead, 5 per cent antimony. Pistol makers had also found that the mechanical action of the automatic pistols also damaged and distorted the lead bullets, so they too resorted to jacketed bullets.

In response to the criticisms of his gun, Georg Luger developed a new 9mm rimless cartridge with a round-nose bullet that he called the Parabellum. In its 9x19mm version, it soon became the most widely-used cartridge, not only for pistols but eventually for machine pistols as well. He then went on to design several other pistols chambered for his

Below: A German machine gun company waiting for the order to advance with its equipment during World War I. The photograph clearly demonstrates the weapon's lack of easy portability.

Above: German troops digging a trench at Argonne in 1915. Zig-zags like the one shown above were inserted to prevent the enemy setting up a machine gun at one end and sweeping the entire trench clear.

new round, most notably the Modell 1904 for the Imperial German Navy. For the first time, Luger included Borchardt's detachable stock to allow the weapon to be fired from the shoulder. Thereby, in conjunction with a longer 150mm (5.9in) barrel and a two-position rear sight, he made it more accurate at longer ranges. He followed this with his most famous gun, the Modell 1908 (usually shortened to the 'P08' or just '08'), which became the standard German army pistol throughout both world wars. One significant version of this was the 9mm Artillerie Pistole, with a detachable stock and a range of detachable barrels, the largest being 200mm (8in). Further versions appeared in 1914 and 1917. The only drawback of the pistol was that it had an eight-round magazine. To overcome this deficiency, a 32-round *Trommel* (snail-drum) magazine, designed by Tatarek and von Benko in 1911, was added. The spring-operated magazine clipped to the bottom of the hand grip. With this, an experienced firer could accurately shoot all 32 rounds in no less than 45 seconds, even though it was still a single-shot weapon.

The development of German automatic pistols was not carried out by Luger alone, for Louis Schmeisser, a gunsmith and designer for the Rheinish Metal Goods and Machine Factory in Sommerda, was designing his own weapon, in addition to a cartridge that had neither rim nor cannelure. He had been part of the team that designed the Bergmann machine gun at the Theodore Bergmann Weapons Works in Gaggenau (later Suhl). At the same time, Theodore Bergmann himself was designing his own self-loading pistols, the first being chambered for Schmeisser's cartridge.

The outbreak of World War I and the horrors of close-quarter combat in the trenches were soon to demonstrate a real need for a light weapon with the firepower of a machine gun. By the end of 1914, despite firepower becoming more important, the theory of mass still dominated European military thought. After the Germans were halted in their tracks at the battle of Marne in September 1914, they went on the defensive and began to dig in. The idea that battles would be won by large-scale mobile operations supported by cavalry charges soon began to disappear as soldiers dug deeper and deeper into the ground to avoid indiscriminate slaughter from machine guns and quick-firing artillery. Instead, the infantry began concentrating on breaking up attacks from their opponents. Foxholes and slit trenches soon became linked together, until they formed continuous trench systems. By then, the machine gun in its defensive role had become the queen of the battlefield, with artillery used to conquer territory, while the infantry had merely to occupy it.

The trenches were normally built 2–3m (6ft 6in to 9ft 10in) deep and no more than 2m (6ft 6in) wide. Into their walls dugouts were built to house the men. To minimise the effects of artillery and to prevent a machine gun being set up at one end and clearing the whole trench, they were built in a series of sections which, from the air, looked like the battlements of a castle. The length of each section was typically 10m (32ft 9in) long and screened from the next by barriers of earth and sandbags jutting out into the trench. They were also intersected by communication trenches, which led back to the support lines and the rear. And sprouting into no-man's land at right angles from the trenches were narrow passages called saps that led to two- or three-man listening posts.

Below: This aerial view highlights the zig-zag way in which trenches were dug. This method also limited the effects of shrapnel from artillery fire. A single communication trench (right) leads to the rear.

Forced onto the offensive, the British and French continued with the mass theory, attacking in waves proceeded by an artillery barrage, up until the battle of Passchendaele in 1917. The barrage often had little more effect than to turn the ground that the men were to cross into a liquid mud that slowed their advance. The Germans, on the other hand, examined their defensive tactics, and with the support of General Erich Ludendorff introduced a defence based on counterattacks that would have the objective of recovering the ground lost. To this end, they reorganised divisions of four regiments in two brigades into more tactically manoeuvrable units of three infantry regiments in a number of defensive zones with an elastic capacity for defending in depth rather than in rigid lines. As part of these changes, tactical control was decentralised so that a squad of one NCO and 11 men became the official tactical battle unit.

VON LOSSBERG'S DEFENCE

From the start, Ludendorff's theories were opposed by Colonel Fritz von Lossberg, Germany's chief of staff. Eventually von Lossberg acknowledged the need for elastic defence and an increased decentralisation of command. It would be the Colonel who would first employ these methods in combat, thereby giving them his name. The von Lossberg style of defence consisted of a forward outpost zone, a main battle zone and a rear battle zone. The forward

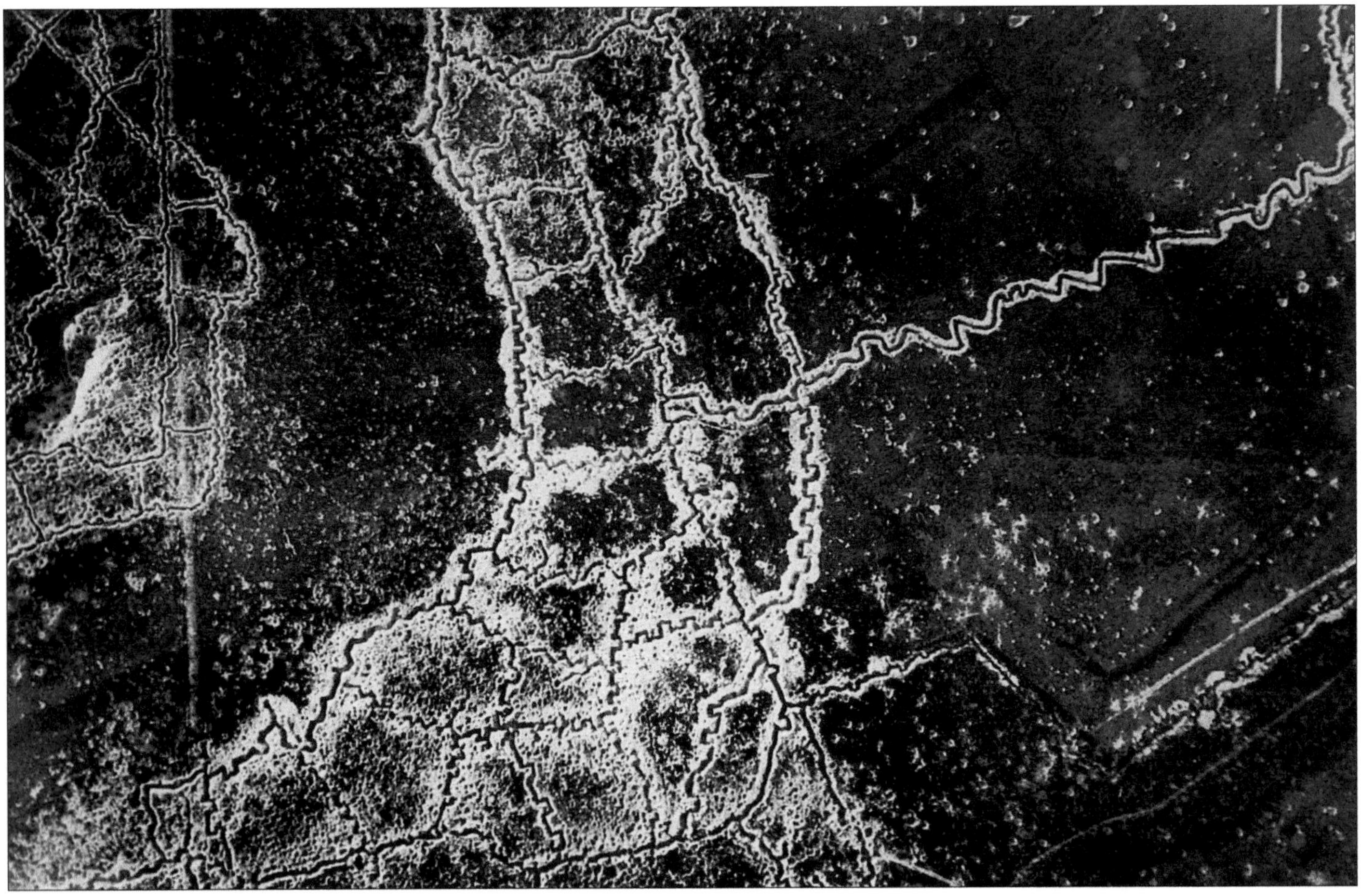

Above: British machine guns – in this case a Vickers Class C on the Somme in 1916 – were no more portable than their German or French counterparts. The gunners are wearing gas masks in case of an attack.

zones were up to 2.8km (1.5 miles) deep and organised into nests of resistance (*Wiederstandsnester*) in a checkerboard pattern of positions. The main battle zone, where enemy attacks were to be stopped, was again around 2.8km (1.5 miles) deep. Behind this was the rear battle zone where the artillery was placed. Counterattack forces in the first zone consisted of small groups of storm troops (*Sturmtruppen*) and in the battle zone of storm-battalion (*Sturmbataillone*) machine guns. Sited initially to break up attacks, they were now sited to support counterattacks. The Hindenburg Line, the backbone of Germany's defences in France between 1917 and 1918, was largely laid out on these principles.

Both sides began to search for a way to break the impasse of the trenches. The Germans soon realised that their tactics in defence could also be put to good use in the attack. Surprisingly, a French officer came to their aid. Captain André Laffargue had written a pamphlet called *L'Etude sur l'attaque* after seeing two machine guns hold up battalions of troops during the attacks on Vimy Ridge in May 1915. In it, he advocated that light cannon should accompany the infantry at the front; machine guns and automatic rifles should also be pushed as far forwards as possible. The first wave of attack should either search out empty space through which to advance, or creep through the enemy defences and take them by surprise. Once the trench system was penetrated, the infantry spread out laterally, clearing the fire bays and traverses one at a time. Laffargue's ideas were on the whole ignored by the Allies, the British not even translating them. However, a copy fell into German hands and, because it matched their own ideas, they soon had it translated and published as a training manual.

It is almost certain that it was Ludendorff who further refined this new approach. At the heart of the German tactics was the high level of decentralisation of command. Unlike the Allies, who still attacked limited hard targets in waves, assaults were spearheaded by small groups of *Sturmtruppen*, who sought out the soft spots in the lines through which they could penetrate until they reached the Allied artillery positions. These storm troops were the youngest, fittest and most experienced from the line regiments. Like the rest of the German army, they were organised into squads of two sections (*Truppen*), the light-machine-gun section of four men (two operators and two ammunition carriers) and an assault section (*Stoss Trupp*) of seven riflemen. In place of the light machine gun they could also carry an automatic rifle and later would be equipped with their own mortar. Around 250m (272 yards) behind them came *Sturm* companies with flame-thrower troops. Their job was to envelop these positions by pushing through the soft spots. Another 150m (163 yards) back came the *Sturm* battalions with the heavy weapons needed to provide fire and flank support to the front-line companies. Pockets of resistance along the line of advance would be further reduced by additional troops following behind. In fact, it was these tactics that would be refined into the Blitzkrieg style of warfare of World War II.

Although the Germans experimented with 'soft spot' tactics at the battle of Verdun, they were not employed fully until 1 September 1917, when the German Eighth Army under General Oskar von Hutier captured the city of Riga in two days. Similar tactics were used at Caporetto and again at Cambrai, each time succeeding far beyond all their expectations.

Below: A 9th Scottish Rifles raiding party waiting for the order to assault a German trench at Arras. Raiding parties usually carried revolvers and sharpened digging tools for hand-to-hand combat.

Much more common than the major attack was the trench raid, the aim being not only to gather intelligence but also prevent front-line troops from adopting a passive attitude. Which brigade carried out the first one is still a topic of debate. However, it is generally agreed that it was either the Canadians or the Indian Gerwhal Rifles late in 1914. A raiding party could consist of up to 30 men who would often spend several days training and preparing for the raid. Before and during the raid, artillery would lay down a box barrage around the attack point to isolate it and prevent enemy reinforcements being brought up. By 1916, the Germans had become very proficient in this type of attack, and called it a 'winkle raid'.

Whether it was raid or a major attack, infiltrating an enemy trench proved to be difficult. At first the men were equipped with the standard rifle and bayonet, but these were soon found to be a hindrance because of the rifle's length and low rate of fire. Its accuracy and range were wasted in the close confines of a trench. The machine guns that had been used to devastating effect on open ground could often weigh in excess of 18kg (40lb). They needed a minimum crew of two and took time to set up. So, once in the enemy trench, soldiers were reduced to hand-to-hand fighting with pistols, grenades and a fearsome variety of clubs and knives.

Above: The Tyneside Irish Brigade attack La Boisselle on the first day of the Somme. The British took 60,000 casualties that day: this photograph shows how exposed the attackers were to machine gun fire.

What they really needed for fighting in these conditions was a compact close-quarter combat weapon that could easily be carried and fired by one man, yet was capable of delivering a devastating hail of bullets, like a machine gun, over short distances. It was to overcome this shortfall that late in 1915 the German Rifle Testing Commission based at Spandau issued a requirement for a lightweight, fully automatic close-quarter weapon, that was simple and robust with a maximum range of 200m (218 yards). It should also be suitable for the existant 08 9mm pistol cartridge.

THE MP18I

The first attempt by the Germans was to convert the long 08 Luger artillery pistol barrel and shoulder stock. However, the pistol had too fast a cyclic rate of fire, and the muzzle had a tendency to pull upwards while firing (known as muzzle climb) because of its light weight. This meant it could not be kept on target. The commission therefore decided to look for a completely new design. It was Andreas Schwartzlose in Berlin and Hugo Schmeisser (Louis' son) of C.G. Haenel in Suhl, who began to search for a solution.

Early in 1918 the Rifle Testing Commission gave approval to Hugo Schmeisser's prototype, which he had developed with the Theodore Bergmann Weapons Works, now at Suhl. The Prussian War Ministry placed an order for 50,000 of the new weapons. Its official designation appears in many versions, including MP18-I, MP18/I and MP18.I. However, MP18I appears to be the most common. The generic name for the weapon was 'machine pistol' (*Maschinenpistole*). The term 'sub-machine gun' was first used to describe the 'Tommy gun'. Even then it did not become universally accepted as the name for this type of weapon until after the end of World War II. After Schmeisser passed the rights to Bergmann, the MP18I also became known as the 'Bergmann' machine pistol, or the Bergmann Muskete.

The *Stosstruppen* (assault troops) who would use it to devastating effect in the 1918 German offensives on the Western Front soon nicknamed it the *Kuglespritz* ('bullet squirter'). The new weapon gave them far more freedom of movement than did the light machine guns they had been using. It was originally planned to establish six machine-pistol detachments, consisting of an operator and ammunition carrier, with 2500 rounds per company carried in a hand cart. However, at the war's end in 1918, only 10,000 machine pistols had been issued. Many were also issued to less well-trained troops who used it like a light machine gun. So despite its success with the storm troops, incorrect use of the MP18I elsewhere created many misgivings within the German High Command well into the 1930s.

Like all other infantry weapons of the day, the MP18I was produced by craftsmen. That meant that it was expensive and time-consuming to produce. Its receiver and moving parts were first forged to approximately the correct size and shape, which then required hours of precision

Above: German storm companies in training near Sedan. Like the submachine gun, the flame-thrower was a new weapon used by the storm troops which proved to be effective in clearing Allied trenches.

machining and hand-finishing to reach the specified size. Each component was meticulously matched to its mating parts, so although each weapon was in itself a work of art, components from one could not be interchanged with those of another. However, weapon operating mechanisms of the period were often extremely complicated, so when the MP18I was introduced with only 34 individual parts (excluding magazine and screws), it revolutionised the art of weapons' manufacture.

SNAIL-DRUM MAGAZINE

The MP18I was chambered to fire the Luger 9x19mm cartridge. Schmeisser's original design included a straight magazine; however, at the insistence of the Rifle Testing Commission, the gun went into production with the 08 Luger's 32-round *Trommel* (snail-drum) magazine. To achieve this, the magazine housing had to be adapted with a sleeve to prevent the magazine interfering with the bolt. To feed properly, it was also set to the same 60-degree angle as the Luger pistol grip. This made the MP18I difficult to handle, so after the war the design reverted to Schmeisser's original specification with a 20- or 30-round box magazine (*Stangenmagazin*) of a double-stack, single-feed design. Because of its smaller size, the new magazine did not fit the existing wartime weapons. By this time, Schmeisser had brought into the C.G. Haenel Weapons Factory in Suhl, and it was from here that he manufactured a new holder that remedied the feed problem for the gun and could be retrofitted to existing weapons.

The main features of the MP18I included the 200mm (7.87in) air-cooled barrel. This type of design had comparatively thin barrel walls that became very hot very quickly. It therefore required a ventilated jacket to protect and cool the barrel as well as to act as a hand guard. It was for this reason that the first part of the MP18I's barrel jacket was perforated with six rows of holes. The barrel itself was fixed into the forestock and was hinged just below the magazine and ejection ports to facilitate stripping and maintenance. It also had a walnut half stock, the same shape as the infantry's standard-issue 98 rifle.

The MP18I fired from the open-bolt position; that is to say the bolt was in the most rearward position before firing. Cocking the weapon pulled the breech block or bolt back, engaging it with the sear and compressing the return spring.

Once the trigger was pulled the sear lowered, freeing the return spring, which in turn rapidly propelled the cylindrical steel breech block forwards. As it moved forwards, the breech took the uppermost round from the magazine, pushing it into the chamber, immediately striking against the barrel end. At the same moment, the firing pin (housed within the breech block) struck the percussion cap of the cartridge, which in turn fired the round. The gas pressure in the barrel and chamber not only forced the round out of the barrel but also overcame the inertia of the breech block and spring, forcing them back into their starting position. Since the 700g (24.7oz) breech block was considerably heavier than the bullet, it moved far more slowly. As the bullet left the barrel, the cartridge case was only partially drawn out of its bed, meaning that the barrel end was still closed. As the breech block moved further back, the cartridge case became free and was immediately thrown out of a window on the right by the ejector. If the trigger remained depressed, the sear stayed open, allowing the breech to move forwards and start the cycle again. However, if the trigger was released, the sear rose, holding the breech block in its (open) start position until the trigger was pressed again. When the return spring was compressed, the breech could be locked by hooking the cocking grip into a safety notch. With one or two exceptions, it was this simple action that would soon be adopted as the standard machine-pistol design throughout the world.

The MP18I was designed as fully automatic only, firing 350–400 rounds per minute (rpm). A 32-round drum magazine could be emptied in 3.5 seconds while spraying a 15m (49ft 3in) arc. The 1918 operating manual describes the use of two types of firing:

- Sustained fire: converging and shifting fire.
- Spray fire: this involved quickly releasing the trigger while firing.

The maximum useful range of the weapon was 200m (218 yards) with the flip-style sight set at either 100m or 200m (109 yards or 218 yards). In reality, under combat conditions, its efficiency rapidly deteriorated above 50m (55 yards) because of the ballistic performance of the ammunition.

VILLAR PEROSA

At around the same time as the Rifle Testing Commission issued their requirements, Abiel Botel Revelli had been working on his own designs in Italy for Officine di Villar Perosa. In 1915 they produced a scaled-down machine gun for use in aircraft and vehicles. During the war with Austria it was used as a light machine gun: in a defensive role mounted behind a shield; and in an assault role by holding it on a wooden tray slung around the firer's neck. The Villar Perosa (VP), as it was known, consisted of two weapons joined by collars. In the place of stocks, it was fitted with two brass hand grips like a medium machine gun. To allow both weapons to be cocked simultaneously, a connecting rod joined the levers through the cocking-lever slot on the right-hand side of each body.

Below: A Stoss Trupp (assault section) of a German Sturm Trupp (Storm Troop) crossing barbed wire defences in 1917. These men were usually the youngest and fittest members of a line regiment.

Bergmann MP18I

1 foresight
2 barrel jacket
3 32-round 'snail' magazine
4 barrel
5 sling swivel
6 chambered round
7 magazine housing

Unlike the MP18I, each breech block was mounted on a rail that curved at the front end. This curve caused a 45-degree rotation of the bolt at the end of its forward motion. It was this turning motion of the bolt that allowed the firing pin to emerge from its front face and strike the cartridge. This not only meant that the round could not be ignited prematurely, but also on the return stroke the friction of the bolt on the track slowed the bolt down, allowing time for the gases to escape. This action became known as delayed blowback. Unlike conventional blowback, there was no need for a heavy

Calibre	9mm (0.354in)
Length	81.3cm (32in)
Weight	4.18kg (9.2lb)
Feed	32-round 'snail' drum
System of operation	blowback
Rate of fire (cyclic)	400rpm
Muzzle velocity	365mps

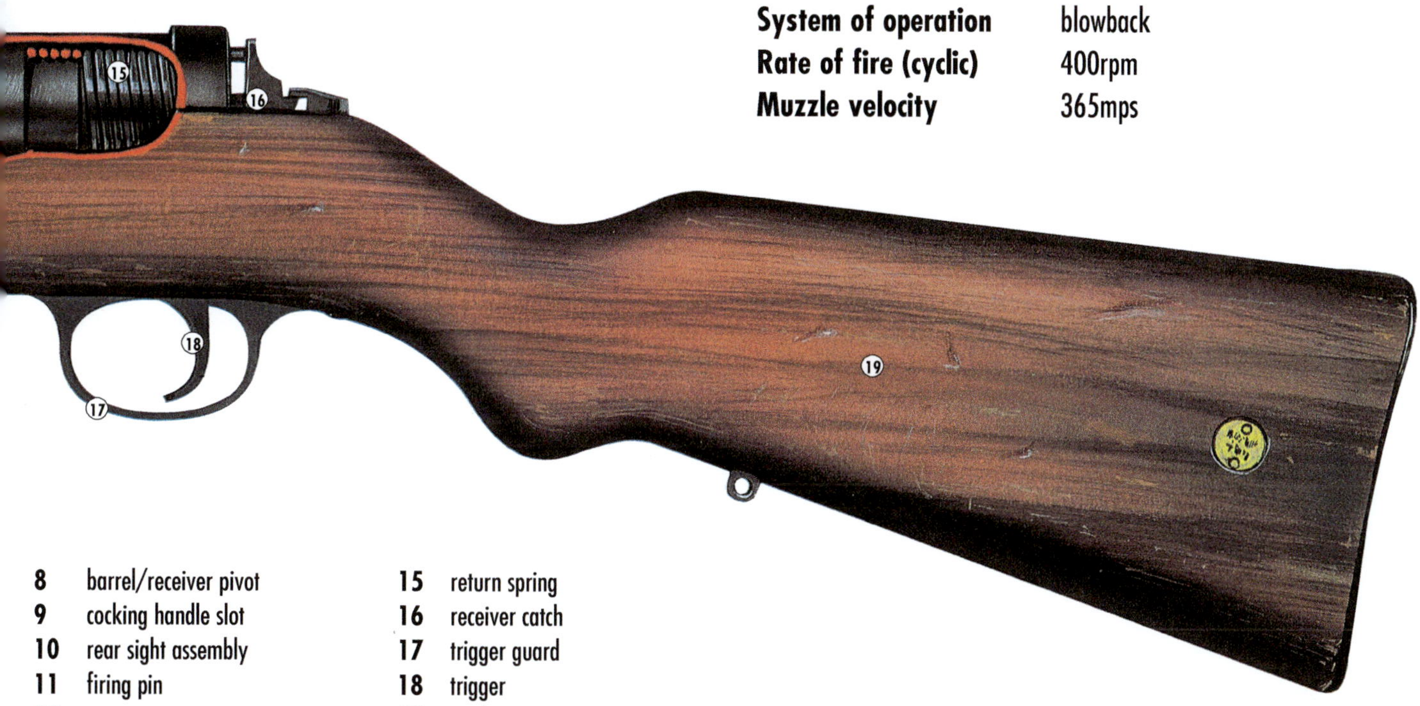

8 barrel/receiver pivot
9 cocking handle slot
10 rear sight assembly
11 firing pin
12 sear
13 cocking handle
14 bolt assembly
15 return spring
16 receiver catch
17 trigger guard
18 trigger
19 stock

Left: A Bergmann MP18I with the 08 Luger 32-round Trommel (snail-drum) magazine, introduced at the insistence of the German Rifle Testing Commission. The cocking handle is visible on its right side.

bolt, although it required a powerful return spring. This led to a very high rate of fire (1200–1500rpm) which made it unpopular with the Italian army. The curved 25-round magazine, open at the rear, was mounted on the top of each weapon. Like the German requirement, it fired a 9mm round. However, the Glisenti cartridge was low-powered and rarely seen outside Italy. It was not until World War I was over that Officine di Villar Perosa issued the VP as a machine pistol by changing to a single barrel, fitting a conventional stock and reducing the barrel length by 400mm (16in), while adding an unperforated jacket.

Meanwhile, another Italian company, Pietro Beretta at Brescia had given Tulio Marengoni, a young engineer, the task of refining the Villar Perosa. This he did by replacing the trigger mechanism with one for fully automatic fire only, uprating the recoil spring to slow its rate of fire and reducing its size. He also added a new stock and an ejection chute under the ejection slot. This new version went into service in 1918 as the Beretta Moschetto Automatico Modello 1918, issued to the *Arditi* (assault units) of the Italian army. However, the debate whether the original Villar Perosa was a machine pistol or in fact a light machine gun and whether it came before the MP18I still rages today.

THE TRENCH BROOM

While Schmeisser and Revelli were developing their machine pistols in Europe, Brigadier General John Tagliaferro Thompson was working on his own designs in the USA. Having spent most of his career in the US Ordnance Department, he had been involved in the development of The Springfield '03 and .30in-06 cartridge and had also been involved in the adoption of the Colt .45 automatic pistol as the M1911. By the outbreak of World War I, he had retired and, in the same year, designed a self-loading rifle. He was convinced that blowback operation was the best method, but because of the need for a high-powered round, he had to find a way to delay the return of the breech block while the pressure was too high. For a solution to this, he looked to Commander John Blish, a retired US navy officer. Blish had noticed that a screw-breech gun remained closed under high pressure but opened when the charged pressure reduced. From these observations he had designed a metal wedge

mounted in angled slots in the body. When the pressure was high, the block was held in place; once the pressure dropped again the wedge moved up in its slot, allowing the breech to return. This patented device was known as the Blish Hesitation Lock. As payment for the use of the device, Thompson offered Blish 1500 shares in his newly floated company, the Auto Ordnance Corporation, based in New York. The other major shareholders at the time were Thompson, who held 10,000 shares and Thomas Fortune Ryan, with 18,000 shares. Thompson had also employed Theodore H. Eickhoff as chief engineer. It was soon found that the only round that worked with the Hesitation Lock was the .45 APC used in the 1911 Colt pistol. It could therefore be no longer called a rifle, so Thompson described it as a hand-held machine gun, a 'Trench Broom' to sweep the enemy away.

With the United States entering the war, Thompson was recalled to active service. Eickhoff continued development of the gun, and with the added assistance of Oscar Payne, the first gun finally appeared in October 1917. Called the Persuader, it was tape-belt fed and included a new version of the Hesitation Lock with an H-shaped wedge. Thompson's Trench Broom also featured two pistol grips. The foregrip was sculptured for the fingers and attached to a flat extension plate that protruded from the front of the receiver below the barrel. Although it did not have a buttstock, the receiver stretched back far behind the trigger to accommodate the long return spring and buffer. However, it failed every trial, primarily because the Hesitation Lock failed to function properly. It took until November 1918, the same month as the end of the war, to have the next prototype ready. This was called the Annihilator and was introduced with a 20-round box magazine known as Type XX.

Left: Unlike the Germans, the British were distrustful of submachine guns, and the standard infantry weapon of World War I, the Lee-Enfield SMLE rifle, was still the primary infantry weapon in 1939.

Above: The French, too, were uninterested in the submachine gun, and would not develop one of their own until the mid-1930s. Here British wounded pass a French outpost armed with a Hotchkiss M1914.

THE BRITISH AND THE FRENCH

The British first tested a Villar Perosa machine pistol in October 1915. They tested an MP18I in September 1918 and sent a report to GHQ France. Eleven months later, GHQ France replied that 'no weapon of the pistol nature can ever replace the rifle as an Infantryman's main arm.' The French held a similar stance until the mid-1930s, when they began to develop their own weapons. However, it was not until the beginning of World War II that the British showed any real interest in machine pistols.

CHAPTER 2

Between the Wars

On 11 November 1918, Germany surrendered to the Allies. As part of the Treaty of Versailles they were prohibited from developing, manufacturing or possessing any new aircraft, tanks or machine guns, and their factories were dismantled. The Inter-Allied Control Commission was set up by the Allies to police the terms of treaty.

Many weapons were either confiscated or destroyed, including a substantial number of machine pistols. The few that remained were only to be used for 'actions in support of a civil authority'. They included a number of MP18Is that could be retained for use by the police in a ratio of one for every 20 men. The army was also restricted to a new defence force, to be called the *Reichswehr*, made up of 96,000 men and 4000 officers organised in seven infantry and three cavalry divisions. The only manufacturer that was allowed to produce rifles for them was the minor firm Simpson, based in Suhl. The *Reichswehr* would soon become a hand-picked force of dedicated, combat-experienced troops divorced from the social and political problems elsewhere in Germany. However, because they were remote, funding for new equipment was not only limited but resented by all political parties of the time. In 1924 a group of *Reichswehr* officers began to re-establish a new armaments industry on their own in secret, even concealing it from their own government. In January 1926, as a front for their activities, the Statistical Corporation was formed under the direction of the industrialist Dr von Borsig, director of Rheinmetall.

Another condition of the Treaty of Versailles required Germany to pay huge reparations to the countries she had invaded, including France who, in retaliation for non-payment, seized the industrialised Ruhr in 1923. The Mauser Weapons Factory (renamed Mauser Works AG in 1922) had to convert production to machine tools and vehicles, selling over 2000 machines to Czechoslovakia and Yugoslavia. Rheinmetall-Borsig AG were more fortunate. They managed to smuggle 2300 tons of tools, materials and production facilities into Holland just in time. All these stores were

Left: An NCO from the SS Totenkopf Division armed with an MP28 leads a reconnaissance section in the Demyansk pocket in 1942. The MP28 was a development of Schmeisser's original MP18I design.

Left: An SS Officer carrying an MP28 on the Eastern Front during the summer of 1941. The gun externally resembled its predecessor, and the main difference was the introduction of a fire selector switch.

hidden in rented warehouses in Rotterdam and Delfzyl under false declarations. Over the next few years, through an Austrian intermediary, Rheinmetall began to buy up all the stock of Solothurn Weapons Factory in Switzerland. By 1929, they were back in their real business of producing machine guns and machine pistols, even if in exile.

The Royal Rifle and Ammunition Factory at Erfurt, which could trace its roots back to 1814, was another casualty, having been forced to dissolve under the treaty. However, in 1922, with the aid of some of his old workforce, Berthold Geipel, one of the state-owned factory's directors, established the Erfurt Maschinenfabrik (ERMA). Here weapons' development continued in secret alongside the manufacture of machine tools.

Although the restrictions made weapons' design and development very difficult, it was not impossible. Manufacture of the MP18I continued illicitly at the Bergmann factory until 1920. Bergmann then granted licences to several other armaments manufacturers, including the Swiss Industrial Company (SIG) in Neuhausen and the Schulz-Larsen Gewärfabrik in Otterup, Denmark. It was in organisations like these that the MP18I was built in several versions for export to other countries. Variations included tangent sights, bipod and tripod mounts, and bayonet lugs. Those built at Schulz-Larsen Gewärfabrik had the magazine feed on the right as opposed to the standard left mount.

THE MP28

After World War I, Schmeisser continued to develop his MP18I design. The result was a weapon that externally looked almost identical to its predecessor, but had several major internal differences. The most important was the addition of a built-in interrupter that could allow single rounds to be fired. The type of fire could be set by pushing to the side a button on the trigger guard marked D for *Dauerfeuer* ('duration firing' - fully automatic fire) and E for *Einzelfeuer* ('single firing' - semi-automatic fire). To increase stability, the coils of the return spring were considerably enlarged. It was also pushed forwards over the end of the firing pin and backwards over an extension of the breech plate to fit it more securely. Forward movement was also limited by the introduction of a collar. The barrel also employed a different method of attachment to the casing. Instead of the notched folding sight, a curved sliding sight graduated up to 1000m (1094 yards) was used. Otherwise it retained the stock, casing, magazine holder and cocking hook of the MP18I.

Right: A lance corporal of the Wehrmacht seen armed with an MP28 during Operation Barbarossa, Germany's invasion of Russia in the summer of 1941. He has a Luger pistol stuffed into his left boot.

Despite the official ban under the Treaty of Versailles, the *Reichswehr*'s Inspectorate of Weapons and Equipment (IWE), the successor to the Rifle Testing Commission, tested the weapon at Kummersdorf in 1925. Although Schmeisser designed a 20-round magazine for the weapon, the Inspectorate requested a 35-round staff magazine. Schmeisser soon found that the spring limited the number of rounds to 32, even if they were staggered. Even then, the friction of the rounds on each other and the housing could still upset the balance and cause misfeeds.

Because of the weapons-manufacturing ban that was still in force, Schmeisser transferred production of the weapon to the Peiper Weapons Factory based in Herstal, Belgium. Here it was given the cover designation of MP28,II (the same comments as to the official designations of the MP18I apply here also) where it was produced in several calibres, including 9mm Parabellum, 9mm Bergmann Bayard, 7.63mm Mauser, 7.65mm Parabellum and .45in ACP, with deliveries going to the Portuguese police as the m/929, as well as to South America, Japan, and China. Spain copied it and produced its own, while the Belgian army introduced it as the 9mm Mitraillette Modele 34. After the Germans overran Belgium in 1940, this was officially redesignated the MP740(b). However, in practice it was normally issued to police, second-line and garrison troops under its old designation. In the late 1930s Haenel started up production again, primarily for export, including to Ethiopia. A total of 3500 were produced from 1939 to 1940, when all production ceased.

THE TOMMY GUN

With the war over, Thompson went back into retirement and continued to develop his Trench Broom. He also coined a new generic name for his family of weapons that would eventually become universal for this type: the sub-machine gun. The Auto Ordnance Corporation's new version was officially called the Thompson Sub-Machine Gun Model 1919 but retained the name Annihilator and developed into a whole series of slightly different weapons. Annihilator I had a belt feed, whereas II was magazine-fed and had a finned barrel. The Annihilator III was further split into types D, E and F. The latter had only 11 parts. To go with the weapon, Payne designed a new 100-round drum magazine (called type C) that was powered by a clock spring. This had a six-armed rotor that drove the cartridges round the drum to the feeder. A 50-round drum (type L) was to follow soon after.

After demonstrating the Annihilator to the US Army and the US Marines in the summer of 1920, Thompson approached Colts to manufacture his gun. Although they refused to manufacture them, they did agree to act as subcontractors, so Thompson placed an order with Colts for the firing mechanisms for 15,000 Model 1921s. He then placed an order with the Remington Arms Corporation for the same amount of walnut stocks and hand grips, intending to assemble the weapon at Auto Ordnance. However, it would take him another 20 years to use up all the parts. By this time, Model 1921 had a detachable butt, annular ribs on the barrel to aid cooling, and a post foresight with a Lyman adjustable rear sight. It could also be fitted with a bayonet, flash suppresser and silencer. He tried every method to gain the weapon's acceptance by the US armed forces, but without success. Instead, it achieved considerable notoriety as the preferred weapon of gangsters and bootleggers during prohibition in America, when the gangsters nicknamed it the 'Tommy gun'.

THE KONEPISTOOLI (SUOMI) M31

Aimo Johannes Lahti, chief designer for Oy Tikkakoski, the Finnish state arsenal at Sakara, had also commenced development of a series of weapons. They became known as the Suomi (Finland) machine pistol. The first, the Konepistooli M22, had a long quick-change barrel and annular cooling rings inside an open jacket. It was chambered for the 7.65mm Parabellum cartridge, which was fed from

Above: SS *Leibstandarte* troops near Pabianice in Poland. The closest soldier is armed with an MP28; behind him is a soldier armed with an MP38. Many early machine pistols were still in service in 1945.

a curved box magazine. However, it had little success and few were made. This was followed by the M26, again firing the 7.65mm Parabellum cartridge. It had a large recoil buffer behind the receiver, which was operated by air compressed during the return stroke of the bolt.

His next model, the M31, was far more successful. Like other models of the time, it had an air-cooled barrel, and an unretarded blowback operation. One important difference, however, was the cocking mechanism, with a straight bolt handle on the right-hand rear of the receiver that resembled – and was operated like – repeating rifles of the time. Cocking it involved lifting the handle upwards through 90 degrees, pulling rearwards, then forwards and down. Instead of the normal one-piece breechblock, the breech was split into two: the breech base, which included the bolt handle and catch stock; and the breech cylinder, in which the separate firing pin was mounted. Raising the handle uncoupled the breech base from its receiver and coupled it to the breech cylinder by a cam on the catch stock. Pulling the handle back then moved the breech cylinder and firing pin behind the sear against the pressure of the return spring. Pushing it forwards then cocked the spring. The final downward movement uncoupled the breech cylinder and recoupled the breech base to the receiver. It was now ready to fire. One of the major advantages of this cocking action was that it did not allow dirt and dust into the action, which had been a problem with the normal method.

Lahti had also chambered the M31 for the 9mm Parabellum, 50 rounds of which were held in a magazine that was divided into two side-by-side compartments by a partition that stopped 30mm (1.2in) from the top. At this point the two separate feeds merged into one. He also took the Tommy gun's drum magazine and refined it into a 71-round magazine. It was mounted onto the M31 by a vertical

extension that fitted into the receiver. When loaded it weighed 2.5kg (5.5lb), but because it was mounted close to the gun's centre of gravity, this did not have any detrimental effect on the performance. The Suomi was produced under licence for the Swedish, Danish and Swiss armies and it was also sold to Norway. After Germany overran Denmark and Norway, some were captured and used by the German occupation forces, who renamed it the MP746(d).

BERGMANN BMK32, MP34I BGM, MP34BGM, MP35

So as not to be outdone by his one time colleague's MP28II, Theodor Bergmann, with the assistance of an engineer called Müller, commenced development of a completely new series of machine pistols that would end with the MP35. Production of the first began in 1932. In an attempt to circumvent the restrictions on machine pistols, it was called the BMk32 (Bergmann Machine Carbine). In reality, Bergmann's weapon was a standard 9mm machine pistol that resembled the 98k carbine rifle, but it had several important differences. Firstly, its stick magazine was inserted horizontally on the right. Secondly, the firing mechanism was almost identical to what was developed by Lahti, though it had the addition of a delayed-action firing pin.

With other blowback weapons, the fixed firing pin protruded from the breech block. However, this could cause premature detonation of the round as it was being chambered. With the BMk32, Bergmann used a small tipping leaver that rested on the underside of the breech cylinder and slid into the chamber rail, its upper joint (called the striking hammer) resting on a flattened section of the firing pin. At the end of the breech's forward motion, the lower joint of the lever dropped into a hole in the breech case. As this happened, the striking hammer drove the firing pin forwards to detonate the cartridge. A further refinement was the ability to select either single-shot or sustained fire by the degree of pressure applied to the trigger. This was made possible by a crescent-shaped switching lever at the limit of the trigger's travel. This meant that with only a small movement of the trigger, an interrupter would catch the breech cylinder after every return, thereby producing a single shot. But if the trigger was fully depressed, the lever would switch the interrupter off, giving sustained fire until the trigger was released.

Further variants were introduced as the MP34 Bgm and MP34I Bgm, differing mainly in the barrel length. The early models were manufactured by Schulz-Larsen Gewärfabrik in Otterup, Denmark, as the Maschinen-Karabiner Modell 1932 for the Danish army and reintroduced to the German armoury after the fall of Denmark as the MP741(d). Later, as the terms of the Versailles Treaty were relaxed, they were also produced by Carl Walther at Zella-Mehlis near Suhl.

Left: SS troops hunting for partisans in the Soviet Union shortly after the German invasion in 1941. The soldier wearing the metal gorget is armed with an ERMA EMP machine pistol.

In 1934 Theodor Bergmann KG, as the organisation had now become known, received an order to supply the *Schutzstaffel* (SS) with their machine pistol. At this time the SS was not a part of the German Army, and it sourced its own equipment. Production of a slightly simpler variant, the MP35I, was exclusively for the SS and manufactured by Junker and Ruh at Karlsruhe. These were marked with the code 'ajf' and occasionally with the SS runes. By 1945, around 40,000 are believed to have been made. For the export market, the Bergmann 32/34 series of machine pistols was produced in a variety of calibres that included 7.63mm Mauser, 7.65mm Parabellum and 9mm Bergmann-Bayard. In 1939 Sweden also introduced a Bergmann MP, chambered for 9mm Parabellum.

ERMA EMP

With the backing of the Reichswehr and in cooperation with the Inspectorate of Weapons and Equipment, a Biberach machine-shop owner named Heinrich Vollmer developed a whole new series of machine pistols between 1925 and 1930. His 1925 prototype, like the MP18I, was air-cooled and featured a 25-round drum magazine as well as a wooden hand grip projecting from the front end of the half stock. For the next model, which came out a year later, Vollmer modified the barrel and removed the cooling jacket, preferring mass cooling. This meant that the barrel was more conical and more strongly made, thereby relying on its mass to absorb more heat energy without damage and protecting the firer's hand. The next incarnation appeared in 1928. This, too, was different in that it now had a 32-round stick magazine inserted from the left, as opposed to the box version. It was in the 1930 model, however, that Vollmer introduced the most important feature. To stabilise the return spring, he fitted a new long breech cylinder that contained half the return spring, the other half of which was contained in a telescopic sheet-metal tube. The firing pin was also elongated to act as a core for the spring.

Eventually, believing Vollmer's machine pistol would not be introduced, the German army finally withdrew its support. Vollmer continued on his own, undaunted. He built around 400 machine pistols in 7.63 Mauser, 7.65 Parabellum and 9mm Parabellum calibres for export. But as these sales

Right: The complex MP34(ö) was designed by Rheinmetall, but to avoid breaking the Treaty of Versailles, was developed by the Swiss Weapons Factory in Solothurn as the S1-100.

Below: The ERMA EMP (centre) was the last of the old-style machine pistols. Large numbers were issued to the Wehrmacht before the MP40 entered service. A suspected partisan has just been executed.

Above:The MP34(ö) was the preferred weapon of the German Military Police throughout World War II. The Steyr Weapons Factory licence-built the weapon in Austria from 1929 until 1945.

did not even cover his expenses, he had no choice but to turn his designs over to a larger organisation for production. So at the end of October 1931, Vollmer signed a licensing contract with ERMA that allowed them to build and market Vollmer's machine pistol under their own name. It became known as the ERMA machine pistol, or EMP.

ERMA made few changes to Vollmer's design. The EMP was made for single and sustained fire controlled by a switch above the trigger guard on the right-hand side of the stock. Like the MP18I, when the return spring was compressed the breech could be locked by hooking the cocking grip into a safety notch. The block could also be secured by a lever on the right-hand side of the receiver. In both the 1938 and 1940 models, ERMA returned to the traditional air-cooling design, the only other major differences being in the weapon's barrel length.

Significant numbers were sold to both the Bolivians and Paraguayans during the Chaco War of 1932–35 as well as to Mexico, Spain and France (3250, with 1540 spare magazines). A large number was also issued to the German border police (*Grenzpolizei*) and to the German Army (*Wehrmacht*) for the SS before the MP38/40. During World War II, captured French EMPs were issued to the German army with the designation MP740(f).

MP34(Ö)

Another machine pistol that made its first appearance at the Kummersdorf tests in 1925 was a Rheinmetall model designed by Louis Stange, and developed at the Swiss Weapons Factory at Solothurn as the S1-100. It was built to the highest levels of craftsmanship, and was probably the most complex machine pistol of its day. Like all the others, it had full wooden furniture and machined castings. The casing was angular on the outside with a round internal cross section. To facilitate maintenance, it had an exact-fitting cover on the top that was hinged just behind the magazine holder. Onto this lid was mounted a curved sight, adjustable to 500m (547 yards). Unlike Bergmann's MP34 and the EMP, the jacket had round holes instead of elongated slots.

The return spring was encased in a tube that was diagonally mounted from the rear of the receiver, through the wood of the butt to the butt plate. The coil spring could then be drawn out through the rear of the stock if required. The connection between the breech cylinder and the spring was made by a guide rod, one end of which connected to the return-spring housing, the other to the complex breech guide that enclosed the end of the breech cylinder.

On the left-hand side of the stock was the selector switch for either single or sustained fire. The cocking handle that resembled a rifle bolt handle could be found on the right. Two other special features on later models were the bayonet mount on the right-hand side of the cooling jacket and a built-on magazine filler. To fill a magazine, it could be inserted into the opening from below where rounds could be stripped from clips. However, because German 08 rounds were not supplied in clips, this served no practical purpose.

In 1929, the Steyr Weapons Factory was granted a licence to produce the weapon. Five years later, it was adopted by the German military as the MP34. However, so as not to confuse it with the Bergmann model of the same year, it was given the suffix ö for *österreichisch* (Austrian). At the same time, it entered service with the Austrian army (9mm Mauser export cartridge) and police (9mm Steyr cartridge) as the Model 34. MP34(ö)s were also exported to Japan, Yugoslavia

Below: Target practice for the Wehrmacht before the war. Aiming a machine pistol firing on full automatic was difficult, and it took practice to be able to control the weapon successfully.

Above: SA and Freikorps meet at München-Oberweisenfeld on 1 May 1923. The Freikorps were a semi-legal paramilitary organisation; the SA were ex-soldiers who had joined the Nazi Party.

and Portugal in a range of calibres. When Germany annexed Austria in 1938, all production at Steyr was switched to 9mm Parabellum. Being the preferred weapon of both the German and Austrian police, as well as being issued to the German army, the MP34(ö) remained in production until 1945.

PISTOLET-PULEMYOT DEGTYREVA PPD34/38

Before the end of World War I, the Russians were at the forefront of small-arms design, having already developed one of the world's first self-loading rifles in 1916. However, the Bolshevik revolution meant that they did not begin a machine-pistol development programme in earnest until the mid-1920s, when Tokarev and several other designers produced prototypes. Within 10 years Vasiliy Degtyarev had developed the Pistolet-Pulemyot Degtyreva or PPD34/38. Externally, it resembled the MP28 and the Finnish machine pistols, while internally it was very similar to the MP18, except for the firing pin being machined into the bolt face. Like the MP18I, it had a heavy-slotted cooling jacket as well as full-length wooden furniture. It also had a screw-off receiver cap through which the return spring and bolt could be withdrawn. One unusual feature of the PPD34/38 was that, to prolong its life, the barrel was internally chromed.

The PPD34/38 was chambered for the 1930-pattern 7.62mm pistol round, which was fed from either a high-capacity drum magazine that was almost identical to the Finnish model or a 25-round stick magazine. Later models of the drum magazine had the extension arm removed because of its awkwardness.

In the period between the wars, the British tested many different machine pistols. BSA also began manufacturing limited numbers of 'Tommy guns' at their Birmingham,

England, factory. In September 1936 the Small Arms Committee were still describing machine pistols as gangster weapons after testing a 1931 9mm Suomi. Even as late as May 1939, there was complete lack of interest of this type of weapon, as can be illustrated in a report from the Director of Artillery to the Secretary of the Ordnance Board. It said, 'Although we are not particularly interested in this type of weapon, in view of the fact that 1000 of this make could be procured at very short notice, we would like it investigated.' Four months later they were at war.

GERMANY BETWEEN THE WARS

Post-war Germany was full of social and political unrest. Unemployment was rampant and inflation was spiralling out of control. Even before the Treaty of Versailles had been signed, there had been demonstrations and a mutiny by sailors of the High Seas Fleet. It had been fuelled by the Spartakus Group (which would later give birth to the German Communist Party). The Communists tried to seize power again in January 1919. However, in a series of bloody clashes, the revolt was put down by a newly formed paramilitary organisation that was known as the *Freikorps*. This was a volunteer force originally proposed by Major Kurt von Schleichter (later to become Chancellor). It consisted of well-paid, hand-picked veterans recruited in secret with contracts that were renewable monthly. Funded by the Army's General Staff, recruitment posters for the *Freikorps* began to appear all over Germany. Soon afterwards martial law was declared, with the *Freikorps,* now being used by the Army to suppress the uprising, becoming involved in violent clashes.

It was during this turbulent time that Adolf Hitler joined the German Workers Party as member number 555. Its name was soon changed to the Nationalist Socialist German Workers Party, though it would become better known by its acronym, the Nazi Party. By the end of 1921 - because they had started to wield too much power - all paramilitary organisations including the *Freikorps* were banned by the German Government. Ex-soldiers who joined the Nazi Party as enforcers had been referred to as the Sports Division (*Sportabteilung*) or SA. Without changing the initials, it was soon to be renamed the Storm Battalion (*Sturmabteilung*) and was little more than the banned *Freikorps* under another name. As Hitler's power continued to grow, he formed his own personal bodyguard from the best of the SA that were loyal to him alone. At first they were known as the *Stabswache* (HQ guard) then *Stosstrupp* Adolf Hitler. Before too long, they would be renamed the *Schutzstaffel* (guard detachment) or as it was more commonly known, the SS.

HITLER APPOINTED CHANCELLOR

By 1933 Hitler had been appointed Chancellor with a promise to end the humiliation of the Treaty of Versailles. Publicly he spoke of peace. However, he secretly prepared for war. By this time Hitler had solved the massive unemployment problem by manufacturing huge amounts of weapons and equipment, ignoring the conditions of the Treaty of Versailles. The same year the name for the German army changed from the *Reichswehr* (state defence) to the *Wehrmacht* (defence force). To enable Hitler to carry out his plans he would need huge amounts of trained soldiers, so in 1935 conscription was reintroduced. All men would now spend a year in the army and a further period of time in the labour corps. That same year, the population of the Saar Basin, which had been under French control as part of war reparations, voted to return to German rule. One year later the German army marched back into the Rhineland, repudiating the Treaty of Locarno, and two years after that Hitler sent his armies into Austria. March 1939 saw them march in Prague, and September of the same year saw them march into Poland. World War II had begun.

Under the tutelage of General Hans von Seeckt, chief of the army command (the *Heeresleitung*), the general staff

Above: Despite their adoption of several types of machine pistol, the emphasis in the Wehrmacht's tactical doctrine remained firmly on the machine gun as the main squad weapon.

of the army (disguised as the *Truppenamt* – troop office) began to examine all the records from World War I in great detail. They found that the theories of *Kesselschlacht* (encirclement), developed by Alfred von Schlieffen, and modified by General Helmuth von Moltke for the 1914 campaign, were basically sound. However, the front-line infantry in the opening days of World War I had outrun the artillery and logistic supply columns. The French had time to mobilise, and the German infantry, exhausted by its long march and desperately in need of supplies, was thrown into confusion at the first sign of a counterattack. The solution, as the general staff saw it, lay in improved battlefield mobility.

TACTICAL DEVELOPMENTS

Having studied the application of firepower, the general staff saw the future of battles as a series of local actions, infiltrations through enemy positions and flanking movements, in which an infantry section, based around the light machine gun, played a dominant role. This would be combined with the principles of *Schwerpunkt* (centre of gravity), *Aufrollen* (roll-up) and *Aufstragstaktik* (mission tactics). *Schwerpunkt*, first described by Clausewitz in the nineteenth century, literally means 'centre of gravity' but in military terms refers to an attack where the principal effort is to seek out the line of least resistance. This may mean moving away from the original line of attack and main thrust more than once. This theory is sometimes referred to as the 'principle of unlimited objectives'.

Aufrollen is an extension of Schlieffen's *Kesselschlacht,* and means clear as you work along, widening a gap and sealing the flanks of a centre of gravity, at the same time disrupting enemy communications and rear areas. The two combined were described in German military literature as 'tactics of space and gap' and characterised as a series of minor actions over a wide area as opposed to a large battle on a long linear front. Whatever the size of the attacking unit (these tactics are as applicable to a section as a division), they had to be capable of fighting independently, including making tactical decisions. This is where the concept of *Aufstragstaktik* (mission tactics) is employed. In effect, using mission tactics means doing without question or doubt whatever the situation requires. This was the responsibility of every officer, NCO and man.

Meanwhile, in the motorised transport division of the Inspectorate of Transport Troops, Captain Heinz Guderian, a former rifle-regiment officer with signals experience, was developing his own theories. Already experienced with the infiltration techniques of World War I, he was convinced that tanks working on their own or in conjunction with infantry could never achieve decisive importance. The tank's effectiveness would only increase in proportion to the ability of all other arms to follow them. In 1929 he was with the German General Staff when it witnessed German armoured experimental manoeuvres. To evade the conditions of the Treaty of Versailles, these were carried out at the Kazan testing ground on the Volga, after a secret agreement with the Russians. Although these experiments were carried out with mock-ups instead of real tanks, he discovered that, for the war he envisaged, radio command was essential. It was the combination of centre of gravity, roll-up and mission tactics, along with Guderian's theories, that would form the basis of Blitzkrieg warfare. In October 1935 the first three German panzer divisions were unveiled, each made up half of tank crews and half of infantry.

One of the most significant questions that arose was how to get the infantryman across what was to be termed 'the last 300 metres' alive. They first looked at the German infantryman's shooting skills and found that under a supporting artillery barrage, defending troops had a natural tendency to shoot high. They also noted that under the same barrage, attacking troops tended to charge forwards to evade hostile shells. By the end of World War I, however, this effect had been negated, because German artillery methods had improved so much that enemy artillery was normally silenced before any attack. The infantry was therefore no longer drawn forwards by enemy artillery, nor could the attacker run under enemy rifle fire. One suggested solution was to arm one-third of the attacking infantry with machine pistols. Lighter ammunition meant that more could be carried forwards to the scene of the battle, thereby ensuring that an ample weight of suppressive fire would be available. As a result, by 1939, all German section leaders would be armed with machine pistols.

THE SPANISH CIVIL WAR

The Spanish Civil War, which began in 1936, gave the armed forces of many nations, including the German Condor Legion, the chance to try newly developed weapons under combat conditions, as well as to test and hone their tactical theories. At the same time, the German panzer divisions that participated in the war further developed and refined the Blitzkrieg tactics which would be used to devastating effect a few years later. One important lesson learned was the value of the machine pistol.

Below: The German 1st Panzer Division on the move during the Spanish Civil War. It was during this time that many of the weapons and techniques of Blitzkrieg were tested and developed.

CHAPTER 3

Machine Pistol Theory

The machine pistol, or sub-machine gun as it is now more commonly known, fulfils a distinct set of requirements and has characteristics that set it apart from the majority of other weapon types, though there is some blurring at either end of the range.

It is a light-weight, one-man weapon that should be fired from the shoulder, although many later models have a collapsible or foldable shoulder stock that can be used to reduce the length for firing from the hip in a close-quarter battle or from the confines of an armoured vehicle. Typically it fires a low-powered cartridge that was originally designed for the military pistol and therefore limits the range and accuracy of the weapon. The trigger mechanism is arranged so that, once it is fully depressed, it will continue to fire automatically until either the trigger is released or the ammunition supply is exhausted. To conserve ammunition and improve the chance of a first-round hit, many machine pistols include a switch that gives the firer the ability to change to single shots. This switch (or selector) operates an interrupter that disconnects the operating mechanism from the trigger by way of the sear after a single round is fired, so that to fire again the trigger has to be released.

RATE OF FIRE

The number of rounds expended during automatic firing is called the cyclic rate, which for the majority of machine pistols is 450 to 600 rounds per minute (rpm). Some, like the early Finnish and Italian models could fire in excess of 1000 rpm. However, this high-speed fire results in a loss of accuracy and control as well as creating ammunition resupply problems. This, considering the magazine capacity and the short ranges over which the weapon would be employed, could leave the firer very vulnerable as he changed magazine. This would also become a problem with slower-firing machine pistols with smaller-capacity

Left: Members of the SS Leibstandarte Adolf Hitler prepare to cross the Gulf of Corinth in 1941. In the foreground resting on the swastika flag is an MP38 with folded buttstock.

magazines, as the German troops using the MP40 on the Eastern Front found out during World War II.

BLOWBACK MECHANISM

Although all the early models were hand-crafted from the highest-quality materials, by World War II the requirement was for a machine pistol that was cheap to produce. It had to be made from the cheapest, most readily available materials and require the minimum of machine tools in the manufacturing process. This meant that it should be of the simplest construction possible and have the minimum number of working parts.

The majority of machine-pistol firing mechanisms are of the blowback type (sometimes called spent-case projection) of which there are two main subtypes. Delayed blowback is the least common. It uses a separate device to hold up the bolt face until the pressure has dropped to a safe level, thereby avoiding the need for a heavy bolt. A typical example of this is the Villar Perosa. The other blowback system is known alternately as 'floating firing', the Becker System (after the German who employed the principle on a 20mm cannon in 1917), or 'advanced primer ignition', although it is more commonly referred to as simply 'blowback'. This is the most common method and is detailed above under the section describing the MP18I. Essentially, the process involves a longitudinal reciprocating movement of the bolt that was powered by the return spring. The bolt normally starts from the rear position to ensure that the chamber is empty and to allow cooling. Otherwise, if a round is still in the chamber, the heat from the walls may ignite the powder in the cartridge, causing it to 'cook off' and fire prematurely.

To enable the bullet to leave the barrel as quickly as possible and the pressure to return to normal quickly, the barrel has to be kept short, in most cases no more than 20cm (8in). This, however, means that the muzzle velocity is low, which in turn affects the range and accuracy.

For a single shot, the maximum effective range of most machine pistols is 200m (218 yards). On fully automatic the range rarely exceeds 70m (76 yards). The main cause of this is the gun's constantly changing centre of gravity, which should ideally be in the bore, but is normally situated below the barrel. In addition, as the heavy bolt moves backwards and forwards, so too does the distribution of its weight. This is further aggravated by the bolt stopping suddenly as it hits the limit of its movement, causing vibration. All this combined causes the muzzle to rise with the first shot, rising further with each successive shot. Additionally, the butt is normally below the barrel, and this causes a twisting movement that pulls the gun to the right. These problems are inherent in all machine pistols and many attempts have been made to overcome them.

One of the first attempts to overcome these problems was the American Cutt's Compensator, fitted to the Thompson 'Tommy gun'. This was a screw-on muzzle attachment that had slots in the top to allow gas to escape upwards and force the muzzle down. Another is the muzzle brake – it reduces the recoil by forcing the gases not only upwards but back towards the firer as well, thereby forcing the muzzle forwards – although this obviously has its own drawbacks.

Below: An unsuccessful recruiting poster for the Waffen-SS asking for Italian volunteers. The figure shown is wielding his bayonet and a rather crudely-drawn MP40 slung around his neck.

THE BOLT

The bolt is the heart of any machine pistol. The most common, simplest and cheapest bolt used is a simple cylinder manufactured from readily available, inexpensive steel. It is bored out at the rear to take the return spring and has either a hole running through the centre to take a separate firing pin or a fixed pin machined on the front face. An extractor slot, ejector paths and feeders are also machined into it. As an alternative, the bolt is machined in two separate cylindrical sections. The rear part has a large diameter to provide the necessary mass, while the front is approximately twice the diameter of the cartridge to ensure that the round feeds into the chamber.

Right: The FG42 assault rifle (centre) was designed to replace the MP40 in the German paratrooper's armoury, but it was not produced in sufficient numbers, and the MP40 remained their mainstay.

Above: Cocking an MP40. The lack of a safety device on the MP38's cocking handle caused a number of accidents, and many were later modified to MP38/40 standard, which had a locking mechanism.

COCKING THE WEAPON

Before a machine pistol can be fired, it has to be cocked. That is to say, it has to be made ready by drawing the bolt and spring back so that when the trigger is depressed, the firing cycle commences. This is done with the aid of a cocking handle that protrudes out of the casing. As it is normally mounted on the rear of the bolt, during firing it moves backwards and forwards in a slot cut in the casing. This slot will usually have a recess cut into the end into which the handle can be slotted to prevent unintentional movement and accidental discharge. On several of the early models this was the only form of safety. The actual position of the handle also varies with the model.

Most machine-pistol cartridges are the same as those used in pistols. The actual choice depends largely on national availability, although the Luger 9x19mm, as developed for the 08 Luger, has become the most common. This has a bullet weight of 8.25g (124 grains) typically with a 400-milligram (6-grain) charge producing a muzzle velocity of around 381m/s (1269ft/s) and a maximum range of 200m (218 yards). The favourite in the USA is the .45 APC (Automatic Colt Pistol) cartridge with a bullet weight of 14.904g (230 grains) and a muzzle velocity of around 280m/s (920ft/s). Although it has very effective stopping power over short distances, it can be inaccurate; the maximum effective range is 100m (109 yards). By way of comparison, the sS cartridge that was fired from the K98k, the standard German rifle of World War II, had a bullet weight of 12.8g (197.5 grains), a charge weight of 2.85g (43.98 grains) and a muzzle velocity of 785m/s (2574ft/s).

THE MAGAZINE

This is the primary cause of any stoppages due to the complexities of design. The ideal magazine must allow easy loading, so the spring must not be too strong, but at the same time it must be strong enough to eject the last few rounds into the chamber. It must also be capable of remaining compressed under full load without failing. Then the housing must also be strong enough to take operational knocks and must allow any dirt or grit to fall to the bottom without interfering with the rounds inside. When fitted it must not move in any direction. It must fit tightly to the weapon and yet release instantly as required. At the same time the opening itself must resist any deformation.

Machine pistols can be fitted with two basic types of magazine: the box (or stick), or the drum. The box type is the simplest, and can hold up to 32 rounds of ammunition in two staggered columns that merge into one at the opening, into which rounds can also be pushed to load it. The drum type, on the other hand, is operated by spring tension. It has to be loaded by removing the magazine cover, inserting the rounds into the spiral guides and closing it again. The tension then has to be applied to the spring by hand. The capacity of drum magazines is normally 50, 71 or – in the case of the 'Tommy gun' – 100 rounds.

The drum can only be transversely mounted below the barrel, possibly with an extension piece. There is, however, far more choice for the box type. A top-mounted box can reduce the amount of muzzle lift by raising the centre of gravity towards the bore; gravity will aid feeding. However, this will restrict the vision of the firer and increase the silhouette. A magazine below will lower the centre of gravity, further compounding the muzzle-lift problems, and its capacity will be restricted to prevent it from being grounded when fired from the prone position or from cover. Also, because it is working against gravity, the spring will weaken quicker. Despite this, below the chamber is the most common position because of the ease with which the magazine can be changed. The third alternative is side mounting. This keeps the centre of gravity vertically constant as the magazine is discharged and has no effect on the spring. However, it does tend to push the barrel towards the opposite side as the rounds enter the chamber.

Right: The MP40 magazine was made from sheet steel. Early designs were flat sided, with later types having two indents pressed into each side. Its neck was reinforced with a spot-welded sheet metal collar.

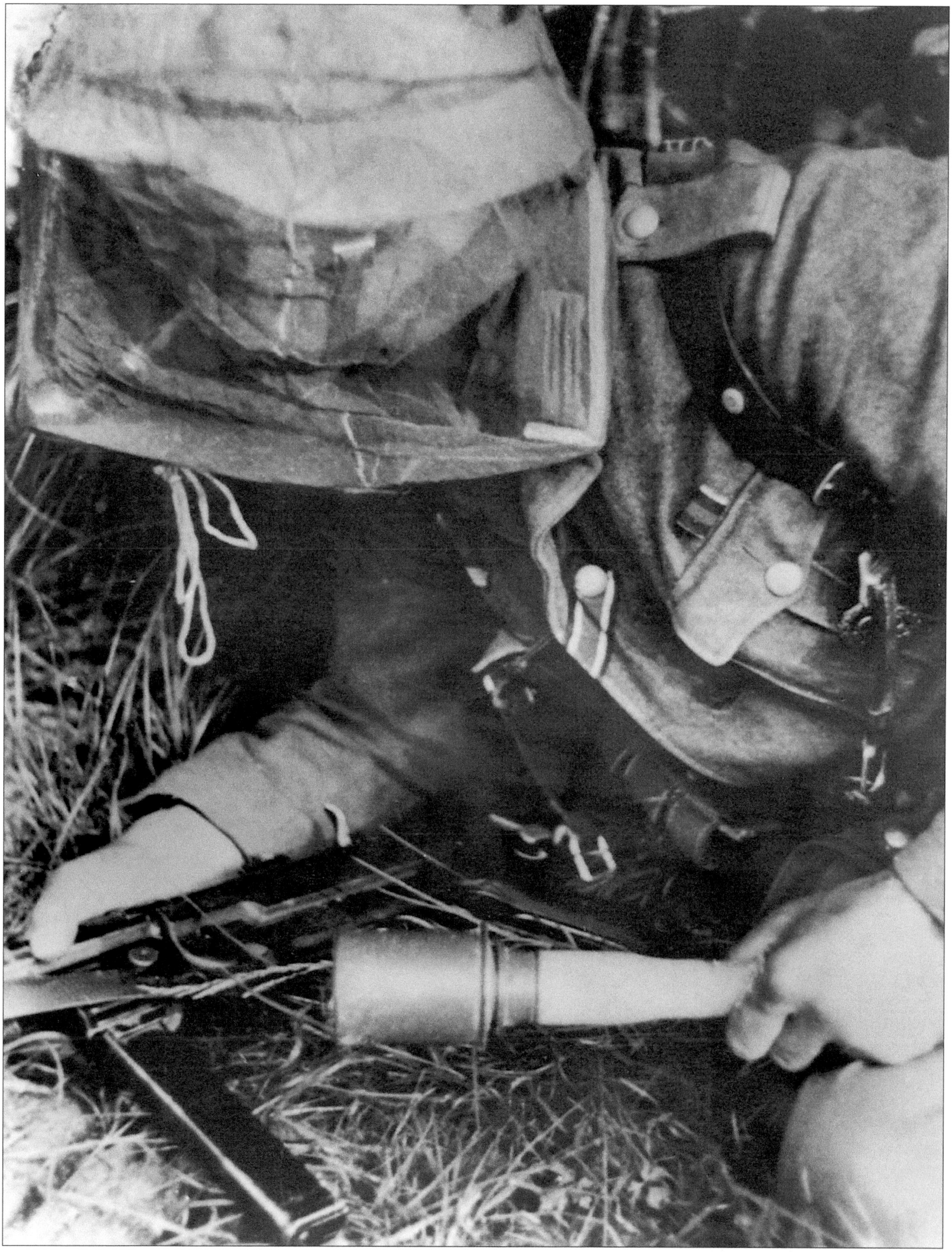

CHAPTER 4

The MP38 and MP40 in Detail

At the beginning of 1938, there were only 7310 machine pistols in Germany's arsenal, and most of these were MP18Is. However, as a result of experience gained in the Spanish Civil War and the new German tactical doctrines, demand for them was rising among paratroops (*Fallschirmjäger*) and motorised infantry.

As a result, ERMA received a request from the German army weapons office (*Heereswaffenamt*), successor to the Inspectorate of Weapons and Equipment, for a new machine pistol. The MP36 prototype gun was already under development, and with a few modifications, it was decided to submit the gun to the *Heereswaffenamt.* The new model was accepted in August 1938 as the MP38, and production was quickly under way, so that by the time the war broke out in September 1939, 8772 had already been manufactured. Although the designer of the weapon is not known for certain, it is generally credited to ERMA's Berthold Geipel and Heinrich Vollmer, as it has several features of their earlier EMP. Production of the MP38 ran until early 1941, initially at ERMA. Then, as more and more were required, they were built at C.G. Haenel as well. Although the exact date Haenel started production is not known, surviving examples indicate it was early 1940 at the latest.

The MP38 was an entirely new concept for machine pistols. It had a free-standing, mass-cooled barrel developed by Vollmer for the EMP. The magazine holder placed vertically below the body meant that the magazine had to be inserted from below. It was secured by a release button on the left-hand side. To make it easier and quicker to insert a magazine into the housing, the end of the housing was flared out and was also designed to double up as a hand grip. Although this meant that the weapon was easier to control and carry, it limited its use behind low cover. Another new feature of the MP38 machine pistol was the folding shoulder

Left: Latvian volunteers in the Waffen-SS on the Eastern Front in 1943. The sniper is armed with a Kar 98k rifle with telescopic sight. His spotter using the binoculars carries an MP40 for self-defence.

THE MP36

Although little is known of its history, by 1936 ERMA had developed the prototype of a completely new machine pistol that was a direct forerunner of the MP38, which it closely resembles. The key differences was that the MP36 had wooden furniture, including the pistol grip, a spring-loaded firing pin, and a two-part bolt joined by a locking screw. Unlike its successors, it was select-fire, the selector being located just above the trigger . It had the characteristic folding stock of the MP38 and 40 that were to follow, though it was not lockable, and the butt plate had grooves machined into it. Unlike all previous designs, the cocking handle is located on the left-hand side. This allowed the firer to keep his hand on the pistol grip at all times. The magazine housing was also unique in that it was canted 30 degrees to the left.

brace in place of the traditional wooden buttstock. This was now made primarily from metal tubing and plastic that, when folded, reduced the overall length of the MP38 to just 60cm (23.6in). To fold it, pressure was applied to the large knurled button above and behind the pistol grip. This allowed the frame to swing down and forwards. The frame pivoted at its centre to lie horizontally below the gun. To save weight, the solid pistol grip behind the trigger was replaced with one made from phenolic resin (a crude early plastic) with paper-fibre filling instead of the traditional wood. A further weight-reducing measure was a circular hole cut into both sides of the magazine housing.

Another new innovation was the bar, with its hooklike projection at the front end of the barrel, which on early models was made from cast aluminium or sheet steel. It has been described as both a cooling aid or a barrel rest to prevent the weapon being pulled, still firing, back into a moving vehicle while traversing rough terrain. Unlike the

Below: German reconnaissance unit in Russia in 1941 wearing camouflage made from bed linen. In the Russian winter, temperatures were so low that metal became brittle and lubrication oil froze solid.

Right: A German squad taking a rest outside Rostov. They are equipped with the standard infantry weapons: visible from left to right are two MP38s, an MG34 and several KAR 98K rifles.

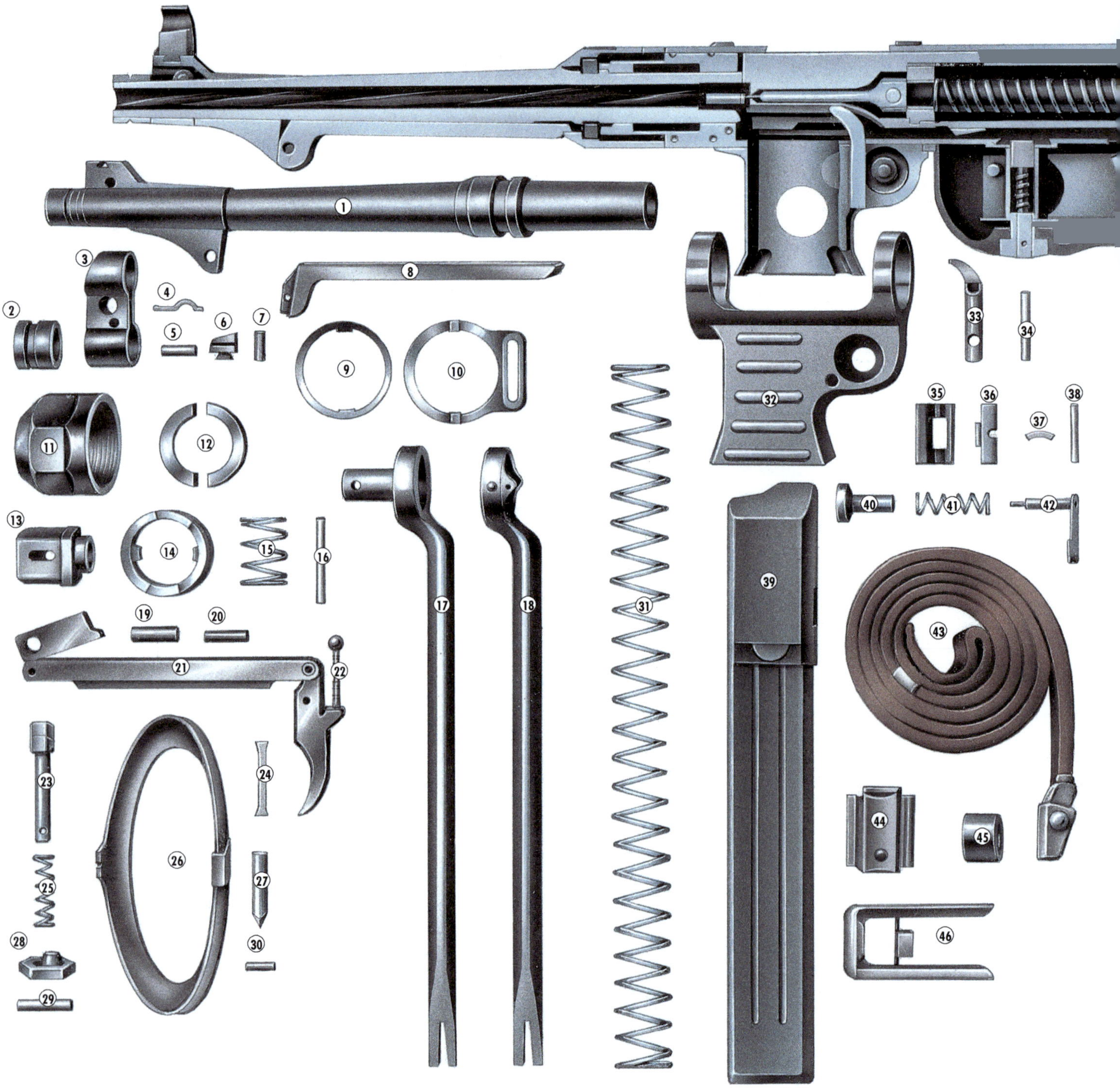

1 barrel
2 barrel cap
3 front sight cover
4 front sight retainer
5 cover retainer
6 front sight
7 resting bar pin
8 resting bar
9 barrel threads
10 collar
11 barrel nut
12 barrel nut washer
13 stock pivot
14 stock release
15 spring
16 pin
17 stock arm
18 stock arm
19 sear
20 trigger axis screw
21 sear lever
22 trigger spring
23 receiver lock
24 bar
25 receiver lock spring
26 shoulder piece
27 retainer
28 dismounting screw
29 receiver lock screw retaine
30 shoulder piece pivot
31 main spring
32 magazine guide
33 magazine release screw
34 washer
35 rear sight leaf
36 rear sight leaf

Erma MP38

37 rear sight leaf spring
38 chamber cover
39 magazine
40 magazine release cap
41 magazine release spring
42 magazine release catch
43 sling
44 attachment
45 muzzle cap
46 attachment
47 buffer spring tube
48 recoil spring second tube
49 recoil spring tube large
50 extractor
51 bolt
52 bolt handle
53 bolt handle pin
54 firing pin retaining pin
55 bolt handle pin
56 bolt handle pin
57 firing pin
58 recoil spring tube end
59 chamber cover
60 pistol grip
61 buffer spring
62 recoil guide
63 recoil guide
64 recoil spring
65 buffer housing
66 fore-end
67 trigger guard
68 lock frame screw
69 grip screw
70 frame screw
71 frame screw
72 grip screw

Above: The MP38 had a free-standing, mass-cooled barrel developed by Vollmer for the EMP. The vertical magazine had to be inserted from below, and was secrued by a release button on the left-hand side.

previous designs, the one-piece cocking handle along with the magazine-release button was fitted on the left. This meant that the firer could change magazine and cock the weapon without taking his hand away from the trigger. However, the only safety mechanism on the MP38 was that the cocking handle, as in the MP18, had to be dropped into a hook-shaped notch in the breech case. In the field this would soon present problems. Many casualties were caused by troops inadvertently dropping or mishandling their weapons, as this would invariably cause the handle to slip out of its slot and fire off a round. While the engineers at ERMA looked for a way to prevent this potentially fatal problem, troops in the field solved it by securing a leather strap in front of the barrel nut and over the cocking handle, slipping it back when they had to fire.

Eventually, ERMA solved the safety problem by supplying parts to the Wehrmacht field workshops, who would upgrade the MP38 by machining a notch into the forward end of the cocking-handle slot in the receiver. Through this a pin could engage and lock the bolt after being pushed through from the other side of the body. This variation to the original design became known as the MP38/40, or the 'mixed model' to the Germans themselves.

The muzzle of the barrel was threaded to allow the fitting of a blank firing device. There was a threaded barrel nut to protect the thread when it was not in use. It would also be fitted with a hinged, flip-up muzzle cap (*Mündungschoner*) to keep dust and foreign bodies out of the barrel. Made of metal, it was attached by an L-shaped catch located on the front of the sight. The sight itself was fixed for 100m (109 yards) with an additional flap for 200m (218 yards). The metal cap fastened to the frame and closing the rear end of the casing was retained from the earlier models of machine pistols. This meant that the casing had to be pulled forwards and out for disassembly.

CONVENTIONAL BLOWBACK

The MP38 was operated by the conventional blowback principle. Its cylindrical breech block was similar to the MP18I and had a three-piece telescopic case that covered the return spring that was of Vollmer's own patented 1933 design. The MP38 was designed for automatic fire only. Because of the weight of the breech and the strength of the spring, the rate of fire was limited to 350–400rpm. This meant, however, that an experienced firer could easily release the trigger quickly enough to fire just one shot.

In addition to the standard model, a prototype light-weight model was also built with both the receiver and body made from one-piece aluminium castings. This was known as the MP38(L), but it never went into production.

Despite all these innovations, the MP38 was still built primarily in the traditional time-consuming manner, by gunsmiths and craftsmen. Many parts, such as the receiver, which had longitudinal grooves machined into the outside to reduce the weight and return spring housing, were still made from machined steel. Even the cover below the body was machined from a cast anodised aluminium, which itself was in great demand for aircraft production. What was needed was a machine pistol that could be manufactured quickly from non-critical materials. This was to come with the next model - the MP40 - and it would revolutionise weapons' manufacture around the world.

MP40

The MP40 was introduced in 1940 and closely resembled its predecessor, with many common parts. Its main difference was in the materials and manufacturing methods. Gone were the expensive machined parts and materials, and in their place were relatively cheap carbon steel metal stampings and plastic, welded and brazed together.

The MP40 is often incorrectly referred to as the Schmeisser. It was probably a faulty Allied intelligence report that led to the name being used to describe the weapon in a US war-department manual of December 1941. The manual, called *Handbook on German Military Forces*, was issued to all senior officers in the field. It describes the MP38 and MP40 as the Schmeisser throughout, which is probably how the name stuck. Although he was responsible for the development of the first true machine pistol, and was possibly involved in the upgrade of the MP38 to the MP40, Schmeisser was by then working on the design of assault guns, so he probably had little to do with the original design of the MP38. However, a 1936 prototype machine pistol designed by Schmeisser does have a passing resemblance to the MP38, in that it was mass-cooled and used Vollmer's telescopic firing-pin arrangement, although it has a standard wooden buttstock.

Like earlier models, the MP40 used a standard open-bolt blowback operation and was for fully automatic fire only. The recoil-spring assembly and guide rod were contained in a telescopic tube. Attached to the end of this tube was the firing pin. Its purpose was to prevent dirt, dust and foreign objects from interfering with the action. This, however, made the firing pin very long and often prone to failure, which was probably why, during 1943, Steyr began producing a variant with an integral fixed firing-pin bolt and a telescopic assembly, but without the provision of a separate pin.

Like the MP38, the pistol grip was made from phenolic resin with paper-fibre filling instead of the traditional wood. The stock, as before, was in the form of a folding shoulder brace made from metal tubing and plastic. The MP40 front sight was of the post type, protected by a sheet-metal hood. The rear sight was of an open U-type notch design and calibrated for 100m (109 yards), with an additional flap for 200m (218 yards). Zero adjustment for windage could only be made by drifting the front sight blade to the left or right with

Below: The MP40, introduced in 1940, closely resembled its predecessor, with many common parts. However, it used plastic and cheap carbon steel stampings instead of machined steel.

the aid of specialist tools. In practice, when the gun was fired from the shoulder, stock extended, the eye was very close to the rear sight but gave a 380mm (15in) sight radius.

Initially, the MP40 still had the old hook-type cocking handle. This would be changed on the next production variant, the MP40.I, when it would be fitted with the locking-type cocking handle that fitted into one of two slots in the receiver. In the forward position, the cocking handle was pushed inwards to lock, while at the rear it was pushed up into a slot marked S for *sicher* (safe). This meant that for the first time the design could be safely carried in the cocked position. Most of the early models would eventually be upgraded to this version. Another modification first seen on this model was the introduction of horizontal ribs to the magazine housing. The purpose of this was twofold: firstly, to improve its strength; and secondly, to give the firer a better grip in wet conditions. Another improvement on the MP38 was that the bar under the barrel, instead of being solid aluminium, was changed first to pressed-sheet steel and then to a phenolic resin. This resin proved to be far superior in absorbing vibration from a moving vehicle. In one later version, the standard return spring was replaced with a cut-down MG42 spring and fitted with an integral fixed pin-bolt. However, this was less reliable and produced an erratically higher cyclic rate of fire.

Below: The thick gloves needed to protect against frostbite meant that it was difficult to put the finger in the trigger guard to fire the weapon. A winter trigger (Winterabzüg MP) was hurriedly designed.

After capturing several MP40s during the North African Campaign of 1942, the US Army rigorously tested the weapon at the Aberdeen Proving ground in Maryland. It was found that the 'Burp gun', as it was soon nicknamed by the GIs, had a cyclic rate of 519rpm using a commercial 115 grain (7.45g) full-metal-jacketed round. After the exhaustive tests that continued into 1943, it was given a score of 79 out of a possible 100. It was further concluded that the accuracy was very good and the general functioning excellent. In comparison, the US-designed M3 'Grease Gun' had achieved a score of 95.

MANUFACTURE

The most revolutionary change to production methods was the use of low-carbon steel sheet in place of machined castings. It was used to manufacture the receiver, the return spring, the magazine housing, grip and trigger frame. The barrel, its retaining bush, firing pin, bolt assembly and the hardened steel sear were the only remaining major components that were machined. The receiver was one of the most time-consuming and expensive parts to produce on the MP38. On the MP40, however, it was simply punched out of a 1.5mm (0.059in) carbon steel sheet and the holes for the sear, ejection port and safety punched through. It was then corrugated by stamping, rolled into a cylinder and fusion-welded along its seam. To finish it, the threaded barrel bush was either brazed or crimped into place.

Three different methods were used to assemble the grip frame. The most common, with a lip around the trigger opening, had the two halves welded at the seam and was then ground smooth. A smooth-style grip without the lip was assembled in the same way. On some later models the two halves were simply spot-welded together, the seams left visible. As a further variation, Steyr also began to produce a one-piece grip frame with integral end cap in 1943. Despite all these measures, and contrary to popular belief, at RM60 (60 Reichsmarks), the MP40 was slightly more expensive to produce than the MP38 at RM57. By comparison, the famous German MG34 machine gun cost RM312. But the major benefit of the MP40 design over that of the MP38 was the ease and speed of its manufacture.

The introduction of the MP40 also brought with it another new manufacturing concept. Because of the simplicity of design, many of the components could be manufactured in any small machine shop, then brought together and assembled by a prime contractor. This would

eventually mean that despite heavy daytime bombing by the US Eighth Air Force and at night by the RAF, production of the MP40 would continue throughout the war.

Above: Two soldiers in a damaged town, armed with an MP40 and flame-thrower respectively. The characteristic pouch for three MP40 magazines can clearly be seen on the belt of the man on the left.

PRIME CONTRACTORS

The three prime contractors for the MP40 were ERMA, Steyr and Haenel (Schmeisser's company). Each manufacturer had its own code stamped on the part, assembly or finished gun to distinguish who made it. They also invariably had a serial number (*Fertigungsnummer*), which, as on all other German weapons, contained an alpha-numeric code that had two to four digits followed by a lower-case letter. The numbers ascend in blocks from 0001 to 9999. The first block has no alpha code, the second block has the suffix a, the third block b, the fourth c and so on. After this was the manufacturer's code and the year of production (the alpha-numeric sequence restarting at the beginning of each year). So, for example, MP40 1567b fxo 43 would be the 21,567th MP40 produced by C.G. Haenel in 1943.

When production of the MP38 commenced, it was still technically illegal to manufacture weapons, so, to disguise the source, they were allotted numerical production codes rather than stamping the name. As an example, all the early MP38s made at ERMA had the code 27. These number codes were eventually changed to letters. Early and late codes for the MP38's and MP40's prime contractors were as follows:

- ERMA: numeric code 27, letter code ayf
- Steyr Daimler Puch, AG Werk, Steyr, Austria: numeric code 660, letter code bnz
- C.G. Haenel, Suhl: numeric code 122, letter code fxo

Although there must have been many small machine shops producing individual parts, the three main subcontractors for the MP40 were Merz Werk in Frankfurt, National Krupp Regestrierkassen GmbH in Berlin and Steyr in Warsaw, Poland. Before the war Krupp were manufacturers of cash registers; their experience must have been invaluable, as along with Merz they supplied the majority of the sheet metal parts. Their identification codes were as follows:

MP38 AND MP40 PRODUCTION 1938–45

Year	1938	1939	1940	1941	1942	1943	1944	1945	**TOTALS**
Army	8772	5700	95,100	139,667	151,033	220,572	217,614	85,869	**924,327**
Airforce	none	none	none	none	66,300	9973	6244	none	**82,517**
Navy	none	none	none	none	12,500	3766	2081	none	**18,347**
									1,025,191

Left: An SBS man shows off his captured MP40 to good advantage. Using a German weapon meant that ammunition was easier to obtain if operating in German territory for prolonged periods.

- Krupp: cos
- Merz: cnd
- Steyr: kur

As all these companies did not start production of the MP40 until after 1940, they have only letter codes.

Another number stamped on most parts of the MP38 and 40 was that of the weapons department (*Waffenamt*) inspector. This was the inspection mark to verify that each part had been examined and found to meet the requirements of the German army. Each factory would be assigned a chief inspector who would be responsible for an acceptance stamp (*Abnahmestempel*) and a team of inspectors. The stamp took the form of the Nazi eagle with a code number underneath to identify the inspector. Some of the numbers have the prefix HWaA or WaA which are the abbreviations for the *Heereswaffenamt* (army weapons department). It would therefore be common for an assembly to have one or more subcontractor's codes, several weapons-department numbers, the serial number, and the prime contractor's code.

Because many of the records are incomplete it is difficult to determine exactly how many MP38s and MP40s were built, although from the serial numbers it appears that at least 1.56 million were built up to 1944.

AMMUNITION

The normal amount of ammunition carried by a soldier equipped with either the MP38 or MP40 was six loaded magazines of 32 rounds each. To load it, the loader first had to be placed over the collar at the top of the magazine with the spring-loaded arm at the rear. A round was then placed on the top of the collar and under the arm. Then the arm was depressed until the cartridge was seated under the lips of the magazine. The arm was then released and the cartridge slid to the rear. This whole process was repeated until the magazine was full. In practice, loading a magazine completely with the special loading tool was difficult and time-consuming, so an experienced soldier would fill the magazine with no more than 28 rounds by hand. To exceed this amount would place excessive pressure on the spring and would cause it to weaken over time. This in turn would mean that a round would not elevate, causing it to jam or the firing pin to fall on an empty chamber.

The exact quantity of ammunition carried per man was calculated by the German high command to be enough for 48 hours in the field. In the early part of the war, at least, the rule was strictly enforced, with all commanders having to make reports of the daily consumption of ammunition by their men. In 1941, the 48-hour allowance for a single machine pistol was 768 rounds. The MP38 and MP40 both fired the standard 08 Pistol, 9x19mm Parabellum cartridge.

Above: A Fallschirmjäger (or paratrooper) rests alongside his MP40. The compact size of the MP40 with its folding stock meant that was ideal for use on airborne operations.

This was a rimless cartridge with a straight case. The jacketed bullet weighed 7.45g (115 grains) and produced a muzzle energy of 400ft-lbs with a muzzle velocity of 390m/s (1250ft/s). In comparison the US .45 ACP bullet weighed 14.904g (230 grains), producing a velocity of 280m/s (920ft/s) and 425ft-lbs of energy. Initially, the German round had a brass case that was marked with a star on the base. In 1940, a steel case with a corrosion-resistant copper or brass finish was introduced to conserve valuable brass supplies. As the war progressed, the finish was changed to green tinted lacquer. To prevent contamination from lubrication oil, the primer on the cartridge was also sealed with black lacquer.

Individual rounds were packed in boxes of 16 each with a light blue label to indicate they were pistol ammunition. A dark blue, vertical stripe further indicated they had steel cases. The label on each box also detailed the type, primer and powder type, manufacturer and date manufactured. Fifty-two boxes were packed into a carton, and five cartons were packed into a case that held total of 4160 rounds and weighed 58kg (128lbs).

There were also several special types of ammunition that could be fired from the MP38 and 40. The 08 mE Eisenkern, with a copper-jacketed mild-steel bullet and steel case, was introduced in late 1940. Weighing only 6.45g (101 grains), it had a considerably higher muzzle velocity. Boxes of these were marked with a diagonal green band. The 08 SE Sintereisen was even lighter at 5.89g (91 grains). The bullet was made from compressed powdered iron. Although acceptable for pistols, the light weight meant that it was often unreliable during automatic fire. The 08 Nahpatrone (subsonic) was developed especially for suppressed weapons. To eliminate the crack as the bullet breaks the sound barrier, the velocity was kept to under 320m/s (1050ft/s) by increasing the weight to 9.0g (139 grains). In addition to these, both the standard and mE rounds were issued in tropical versions (08 Trop and mE Trop). To keep the damp out of these, the primer was sealed with lacquer and the bullet sealed to the cartridge case.

ACCESSORIES

The MP40 magazine was made from sheet steel. It was of a double-stack single-feed design and when fully loaded it weighed 625g (22oz). Early designs were flat-sided while later ones had two indents pressed into each side. The top of each magazine was reinforced on three sides with a sheet-metal collar which was plain-flat sided and spot-welded to the housing. Later it had two horizontal pressed ribs for extra strength. An alternate method of manufacture appears to have been to machine them from a block and these are thicker in section. All designs were marked MP38 u.40, with the manufacturer code and the last two digits of the year.

To carry the magazines, the firer was issued with two pouches, each with three compartments in which a magazine could be kept. The pouch would also hold a small pull-through brush (*Reingungsbürste* MP) for cleaning the magazine interior. On one of the pouches there was an additional smaller pocket that held the loading tool (*Magazin Füller*). This tool was stamped from sheet steel, and had a spring loaded arm that snapped into place over the top of the magazine. Without the loading tool, it was

Below: Fallschirmjäger preparing for the invasion of Crete. The soldier on the left is stripping and checking his MP38 before take-off – a vital precaution against it jamming in combat.

difficult to fill the magazine to capacity. It was stamped from sheet steel with a spring-loaded arm and snapped into place over the top of the magazine. Initially, the magazine pouches were made of dark brown leather, but as the war progressed they were made from heavy cotton with leather strapping. These were attached to the front of the soldier's belt at a slight angle to allow easy access. For paratroops, two special versions were developed that could be worn across a soldier's chest. They were both single pouches split into six compartments. One had a single flap covering all the compartments. On the other, each magazine compartment had its own separate flap, held closed by a leather strap.

The MP38 and 40 normally hung around the neck by its sling (*Trageriemen*), about waist high. At the front of the weapon the sling was attached by a metal loop on the right (or left) side of the receiver behind the barrel nut, while it was attached at the rear by a slot on top of the grip frame. It was normally made from either plain or cross-hatched leather with metal fittings. To protect the end of the barrel and stop the ingress of dirt and bad weather in the field, the MP40 came with a push-on rubber muzzle cap (*Mündungs-kappe* MP). This type was much simpler and far less expensive than that of the MP38, and several were issued per gun.

Another innovation was designed specifically for the freezing conditions encountered on the Eastern Front. It was found that when the firer was wearing thick gloves, he could not get his fingers inside the guard to pull the trigger. A winter trigger (*Winterabzüg* MP) was therefore developed. This was made from sheet metal with a plate fitting over the whole of the trigger opening, boxing it in. On the outside of the plate was a lever that operated like a trigger. This was linked to another lever that pivoted against the actual trigger, so that sliding the outside lever back applied pressure to the trigger and fired the weapon.

Above: Pulling out and giving the receiver-locking knob a quarter turn was the first stage in stripping the MP38 and MP40. This released the receiver and trigger housing, enabling them to be separated.

In 1943, for use by German special forces, Arado of Brandenberg and Schneider-Opel of Berlin both demonstrated silencers (*Schalldämpfer*) for the MP40. Produced in limited numbers, they were designed to be used in combination with the special Nahpatrone cartridge. Although the programme remained secret, its value was questioned by the German high command, considering that the noise made by the bolt closing could not be easily quietened.

Although no blank ammunition was known to have been produced for the army, there was a blank firing device (*Platzpatronegerät* MP) that screwed onto the muzzle. It worked by restricting the gas pressure leaving the muzzle, so that it would cycle with blank ammunition. Another strange device tested was a bent barrel, which was intended to fire around corners. This, however, was unsuccessful in trials and progressed no further than the prototype stage.

The Soviet PPD40 and PPSh41 machine pistols' 71-round magazines gave them an advantage over the MP40, whose magazine needed changing after only 32 rounds. The Germans decided to develop a new version of the MP40. It first went into production in March 1942, though it did not appear on official listings until July 1943, as the MP40.II, with the instrument number (*Gerätnummer*) 3004. The MP40.II was unique in that it had a magazine housing that accepted two standard magazines at the same time. After one was emptied, releasing a latch at the front of the housing allowed it to be moved to the side, while the full one was slid into place with the aid of a guide. Very few of this variant were produced. Weighing an extra 1kg (2.2lbs) more than the standard model, they proved unpopular with the troops.

FIRING THE MP40

To fire the MP40 from an empty chamber and no magazine, holding the weapon by the pistol grip, the firer first had to retract the cocking handle and lock it into the safety notch with the left hand. Then with the right hand still on the pistol grip, he could safely insert the magazine. This in itself was not as straightforward as it sounds. Because the gun's weight was towards the front, it tended to pull the muzzle downwards. It was therefore difficult to hold the gun up while inserting the magazine with the left hand. In practice, this was normally overcome by hanging the MP40 around the neck by the sling and gripping the extended stock between the waist and elbow. After this, the handle could be removed from its notch and eased forwards until it stopped a few inches from the chamber.

To fire from the hip, standing or kneeling, the firer tucked the extended stock between his elbow and ribs on the right side, then gripped the magazine housing (never the magazine itself) in his left hand while pulling his upper left arm into his chest for support. Holding the pistol grip with the right hand, he could then pull the trigger. The MP40's muzzle had a natural tendency to pull downwards. Although a disadvantage when loading, this actually helped to minimise the muzzle climb and any pulling to the right. However, for the best accuracy and for comfort in this position, it was best to use the sling. Detrimental to accuracy when firing, either from the hip or shoulder, was the sensation of the

Below: To separate the receiver and trigger housing, hold the pistol grip and depress the trigger, while twisting the receiver through 80 degrees and pulling it forwards.

heavy bolt's long movement and its slamming into the stops with considerable force as it reached the limits of its travel. But, because of the low power of the cartridge fired by the MP40, there was little recoil.

STRIPPING THE MP40

Before the MP40 could cleaned or repaired, it had to be stripped down. For cleaning while in action only the most basic of strips had to be performed, and it did not require any special tools. This was normally termed a 'field strip'. Usually, repairs meant a detailed strip and this could only be carried out with specialist tools.

The field strip was carried out by first ensuring that the magazine had been removed and the chamber was empty. Then the receiver-locking knob under the body was pulled out and given a quarter turn to ensure it stayed out. The receiver and trigger housing could be separated by holding the pistol grip and the magazine housing while pulling the trigger then twisting the receiver through 80 degrees and pulling it forwards. Next, by holding the cocking handle, the bolt assembly could be slid back and removed from the receiver. Once this had been done, the return-spring tube and firing pin could be removed from the bolt. The gun was then in a position to be fully cleaned.

If a full strip was required, then the above drill could be continued by first undoing the barrel nut and removing the barrel. At the same time, as the nut was loosened, the barrel had to be pulled forwards to prevent interference with the bar under the barrel. After this, the pistol grip could be removed by undoing the screw in the centre of the grip. The weapon was then turned upside down and the small locking screw on the front of the trigger guard was removed. After the larger screw was removed, the grip frame could be separated from the trigger housing.

After this, the plastic arm was removed from the trigger housing, then turned over to turn the disassembly knob, exposing the pin of the knob. Before the knob could be removed, the pin had to be freed by tapping it out with a punch. Then the shaft and spring could be removed from inside the trigger housing. To remove the final plastic housing, the two arms held by screws had to be removed. For the final part of the disassembly the sear and trigger assembly was removed. However, in practice this was difficult without damaging the frame.

Below: The four main components of an MP40 after a field strip (clockwise from top): the receiver; the magazine; the trigger housing and the return spring tube.

CHAPTER 5

The MP40 in Combat

Among the first units to use the MP38 in combat were the newly formed paratroop regiments (*Fallschirmjäger*). When, as part of Operation *Weserübung,* Germany simultaneously attacked Norway and Denmark in April 1940, it was the paratroops who spearheaded the opening assaults. Their task was to capture the main airfields to allow other troops to be flown in.

To accomplish this, they were flown to the target in Ju52 transport aircraft before parachuting in. Their weapons, including MP38s, were dropped separately in containers that had been slung under the aircrafts' wings. Surprise was on their side, and within hours the airfields were secured. Within weeks the paratroops were in action again as part of the glider-borne assault on the Belgian fortress complex, Eben Emael. This was the cornerstone of Plan Yellow (*Fall Gelb*), Hitler's invasion of the Low Countries and France.

At the outbreak of World War II, a paratroop company (*Fallschirmjägerkompanie*) consisted of a company platoon (*Kompaniezug*) and three rifle platoons (*Schützenzüge*). Each of these platoons was made up of three squads of 10 men, equipped with two MG34s and six rifles. Unlike other German units, because of their 'elite' status, each squad was equipped with two MP38s.

To capitalise on the assault on Eben Emael and on Operation *Niwi* (an air landing by elements of *Infanterie-Regiment Grossdeutschland* behind the front line), it was essential that the main army link up with the assault troops as soon as possible. Before this could be done, a number of bridges along the frontier had to be captured intact. One such bridge was the Gennep railway bridge over the River Meuse, which lay 5km (3 miles) inside the Netherlands. The task of taking the bridge was given to an eight-man assault unit of the *Brandenburg* Regiment, Nazi Germany's equivalent of the British SAS or American Green Berets.

Left: An MP40-armed SS Fallschirmjäger shelters behind a wrecked Russian T-34 in eastern Germany, 10 January 1945. His colleague is carrying a Panzerfaust anti-tank rocket.

Above: The Fallschirmjäger were amongst the first to use the MP38, and they continued to use both it and the MP40 throughout the war. The photograph shows three Fallschirmjäger in Rome in 1944.

On the morning of 10 May 1940 two of the men, disguised as Dutch military police, escorted six German 'prisoners' to the bridge. The compact size of the MP38 meant it could be strapped to the chests of each of the 'prisoners', hidden under a greatcoat. Within moments they had overpowered the guards on the German side of the bridge and severed the detonation wires for the demolition explosives. Once they had informed the guards on the Dutch side that they were crossing with prisoners, the telephone connections were cut. At the other side, the Dutch escorted the 'prisoners' away in a truck. The still-disguised Germans who remained behind captured the surviving guardhouse with support from the rest of their unit. A German armoured train, closely followed by a troop train, then crossed the bridge. Meanwhile the 'prisoners' escaped their captors and attacked several Dutch strongpoints along the river, taking 40 prisoners themselves.

Three days later the men of *Infanterie-Regiment Grossdeutschland* were poised on the western edge of

Sedan to cross the River Meuse and move into the heart of France. Sedan itself was heavily defended with an average of eight pillboxes per 200m (220 yards) of front. However, *Grossdeutschland*'s objective lay a further 6.5km (4 miles) to the south: the Marfee Heights, and in particular Point 247. Led by their 2nd Battalion, they relentlessly pushed forwards. For the preceding five hours Germany's flying artillery, the Stuka, dive-bombed the defenders, forcing them to keep their heads down, while the whine of their sirens, nicknamed the 'Trumpets of Jericho', threw the defenders into panic. Once across the river, the Germans were soon at the base of the heights. *Oberleutnant* von Coubiere described the final stages of the assault in *Mit den Panzern im Ost und West*, written by General Heinz Guderian:

> *They climb the slope, through deeply cratered countryside, cross deep barbed wire barriers until the French open heavy defensive fire from behind the ridge. Machine guns and machine pistols send out their death-bringing bullets. Hand grenades explode; nobody pays any attention to the enemy fire. There is no time to stop. The leading troops are already in the enemy's position. Close-combat fighting, hand to hand - with a wild swing the attack is driven forward.*

THE INFANTRY SQUAD 1940

The MP38 and 40 first began to appear in the hands of the front-line German infantry divisions in 1940. At this time a division was made up of three infantry regiments, an artillery regiment with a signals battalion, an engineers battalion, a reconnaissance battalion and an antitank battalion. Each of these regiments had three infantry battalions of four companies each. In turn, each of these companies were split into three platoons.

At this time a platoon consisted of a platoon headquarters and three squads, each of 10 men, though by 1943, because of manpower shortages, the squad was reduced to nine men. The size of a company was also reduced to 80. In some instances it was as low as 40. Apart from the decreasing numbers of available troops, this reduction in numbers was due to the observation that bigger units suffered greater losses without achieving more effective fighting capabilities. Another reason was that junior officers were finding it difficult to control the larger units.

During the inter-war period a considerable amount of time had been devoted to questions of firepower. It had been concluded that the key to success on the battlefield was the light machine gun. As the enemy would only be in view for seconds at a time as they moved between cover, it should be able to deliver the maximum number of bullets in the shortest possible time. To this end, in 1936 the Germans developed the MG34, which had the equivalent firepower of 20 riflemen. By 1939, the German infantry manual emphasised surprise, with mobility and manoeuvre as the method to achieve it.

Above: Although this Fallschirmjäger's MP38 is only just visible slung over his shoulder, his triple-magazine pouch can clearly be seen on his right side, while he also carries a pistol and a stick grenade in his belt.

As discussed earlier, it was envisaged that a battle would be fought as a series of local actions that would expand. Even in the largest battle, the squad was expected to perform outflanking manoeuvres wherever possible. From these two concepts, the squad, built around the MG34, with the remaining members of the squad supporting it and carrying ammunition, became the basic building block of any action. This was in total contrast to an American squad, where it was the riflemen who were the base of fire, and the Browning Automatic Rifle (BAR) the support.

The structure of the squad would remain essentially the same throughout the war for all arms and formations within the SS, the infantry and the paratroop regiments:

The squad leader (*Gruppenführer*). His main role was to direct the fire of the MG34 (later the MG42) and the riflemen. He was responsible for the carrying out the mission itself, the condition of the equipment and ammunition supplies. Because the squad leader would be directing the squad's battle, his own weapon was the machine pistol. Its limited range meant that it would only be used for very close-quarter combat.

The gunner (*erster MG Schütze*). He was responsible for firing and maintaining the MG34 and was the leader of the MG section. Although all members of the squad could fire the weapon, he was picked for his marksmanship.

The assistant gunner (*zweiter MG Schütze*). He was often called 'Zwo', a corruption of *zwei*, the German word for 'two'. His only weapon was a pistol. He carried 200 rounds in four drums, plus another 300 rounds in an ammunition box, and a spare barrel. His role was to supply the MG with ammunition. When his own supply ran out, he would take additional rounds from the ammunition soldier. Normally, if there was sufficient cover, he would lie beside or behind the gunner, ready to take over if necessary.

The ammunition soldier (*dritter MG Schütze; Munitionsschütze*). His role was to supply ammunition, refill drum magazines and to ensure the quality of the cartridges to be

Below: The crew of a 2cm flak gun mounted on a half-track in July 1943. The commander of a detachment like this would usually carry an MP40 for self-defence. His men are armed with the Kar 98K rifle.

fired. In combat he would lie behind the MG. His weapon was the K98 rifle and, if necessary, he would fight as a rifleman.

The riflemen (*vierter bis neunter Gewehrschützen*). The most senior rank of these was the deputy squad leader (*Truppführer*), who led the rifle section (*Schützentrupp*) in battle. Their role was support for the MG and close-quarter combat with the rifle, bayonet and grenades.

In 1943 the US Military Intelligence Service published a manual called *The German Squad in Combat*. It was a translation of an early-1940s German army handbook. It describes the personal qualities needed by a squad leader, such as a stronger will than the men, a disregard of self in accepting privations and dangers, an exemplary bearing before his men in moments of danger, calmness and certainty while being a stern father and kind mother. The role of the squad leader can be summed up by comments made by a Luftwaffe mechanic who had been transferred to the 16th Division during the fighting around Caen: 'I could not see the sea but knew there was a big armada out there, with battleships shelling us...I was so frightened I just wanted to curl up and hide. But we had a loud-mouthed NCO behind us with a machine pistol and he kept driving us on.'

THE SQUAD ASSAULT

An assault by an infantry squad was normally carried out in three phases. First they had to get as close as possible to the enemy position without firing, using all available cover and concealment. If necessary, they made detours to conserve all their shock effect until the final assault. Immediately before and during the assault, the enemy had to be subjected to the greatest volume of fire by all available weapons. This was known as the pin-down (*niederhalten*) phase of the firefight. In the second phase the assault troops infiltrated forwards. Finally, the enemy position was saturated with fire as the assault troops destroyed it in detail. The squad manual describes how 'with hand grenades, machine pistols, rifles, pistols and spades and shouting "Hurra!",' the men charge the enemy positions. 'The whole squad takes part in the hand to hand fighting.'

During the second and third phases, the platoon leader (*Zugführer*) could order one squad to support another. The supporting squad concentrated its fire upon the point of penetration or the enemy's flanks, or rear of where the assault was to take place. All the squad's weapons were employed, even the machine pistols at close ranges.

THE SQUAD IN DEFENCE

In defence, a platoon (*Zug*) typically had a frontage of 200–300m (220–330 yards) with 30–40m (33–44 yards) per squad. This was considered the maximum distance over which a squad leader could control his men in combat. Any gaps between adjacent squads had to be covered by fire. The squad leader would first select a position for the MG that would provide the most effective field of fire. Often, several alternative positions at least 50m (55 yards) away from each other were chosen as well. The remaining riflemen would then be grouped in pairs, usually in ditches or foxholes in a staggered or echeloned formation. These positions also had to be sufficiently close to each other for the men to be able to hear and understand each other even in combat. If time allowed, a second set of camouflaged foxholes were prepared to the rear where the men could wait until a firefight occurred. The American handbook explains that the enormous increase in German rapid-fire automatic weapons (including machine pistols) had so greatly increased their defensive power that well-concealed and covered positions organised in depth might be successfully attacked only by the closest coordination and full cooperation of all arms.

Left: An Afrika Korps NCO sheltering with his men from an Allied bombardment in Tunisia in 1943. Like all squad leaders, he is armed with an MP40.

When attacked, while the enemy were at a distant range, the artillery and the company's heavy MGs would be used first. The squads would stay hidden until they could employ their own weapons effectively and against targets that could not be engaged by the heavy weapons and artillery. Once the enemy was within range, the squad leader would direct the fire of the MG and his squad. Only at very close ranges would he use his machine pistol.

It was not always foxholes that the Germans used to prepare their defensive positions. In May 1944, at Albaneta in Italy, German paratroops made good use of Allied tank wrecks, turning them into well-camouflaged strongpoints. As they had been taught, they let the attackers get very close and then mounted strong counterattacks with only handfuls of men equipped with MGs, grenades and machine pistols. It was these strongpoints that held up the advance of the Polish II Corps and US II Corps through Italy immediately after Cassino. It took considerable effort and cost the lives of many men to dislodge the tenacious paratroops.

A light (*Jäger*) company of December 1943 was equipped somewhat differently. Because of its role, it had no heavy weapons. Like a standard company, it had three platoons each with an establishment of three squads. In each of these, with the exception of the MG sections, all the men (including the NCOs) carried machine pistols.

PANZER GRENADIERS

Each panzer division, in addition to a brigade of 561 tanks, had a brigade of motorised infantry comprised of one regiment of three infantry battalions and a motorcycle battalion. These would later be increased to two regiments of two battalions each. Motorised infantry divisions were smaller than those of the ordinary infantry although they were still organised like a standard division. The major difference was that all elements were transported by vehicle. Later in the war these motorised divisions would be upgraded to semi-armoured status and renamed panzer grenadiers.

In November 1943 a standard panzer grenadier company had a total compliment of three officers, 44 NCOs and 178 men. Headquarters comprised the company commander, a section leader (NCO) and two vehicle squad leaders, plus a driver, all with machine pistols. There was a panzer destroyer section comprising four, two-man crews of a firer and a loader. Each firer was armed with a machine pistol. Then there were four infantry platoons of three squads each. In a motorised unit there was one two-ton truck per squad, while in an armoured company each squad travelled in a SdKfz 251/1 half-track. To support the infantry platoons there were two heavy machine-gun squads and a mortar squad. Each of the five NCOs and the three drivers had a machine pistol for self-defence. A fourth squad of eight men, each with a machine pistol, was mounted in two SdKfz 251/9s with 75mm guns.

As in all other formations, the standard infantry panzer grenadier squad consisted of 10 men under the command of a squad leader armed with a machine pistol. Second in command was the deputy squad leader (or section leader), equipped with a rifle. Two on-board MGs were each crewed by two men, who would take their weapons with them when they got down from the vehicle. The remainder of the squad was composed of four riflemen, a driver and his assistant. A second machine pistol was carried on board each of the vehicles. It was only to be removed on the orders of the squad leader.

By April 1944, the complement of a panzer grenadier company had been reduced to three officers, 29 NCOs and

Right: A squad leader from the Waffen-SS Germania regiment (part of the Wiking Division) identifies targets for and directs the fire of an MG34 team on the Eastern Front in the summer of 1942.

Above: A lieutenant passes orders to his platoon NCO in the mountains of Italy in 1944. The NCO carries his MP40 high on his chest so that he can grip it tightly when firing, in order to limit muzzle climb.

115 men in three infantry platoons, a heavy platoon, two heavy machine-gun squads and a mortar squad. By November 1944, although a tank-destroyer squad remained, the heavy-weapons squads were deleted. In addition, the first platoon of a company was reorganised as a storm platoon, its three squads equipped entirely with machine pistols. At this time, the Germans had begun to introduce the assault rifle as a replacement for both the rifle and machine pistol. However, production of these revolutionary weapons was very limited, so many machine pistols were still in service by the end of the war. By April 1945, the German army was simply running out of men. As a consequence, the complement

of the panzer grenadier company had fallen even further, to 23 NCOs and just 63 men organised into only two platoons and without any heavy-weapons or antitank support at all.

THE EASTERN FRONT

On the morning of 22 June 1941, Germany invaded the Soviet Union. Although many Red Army units disintegrated under the onslaught, many more resisted the advance. However, this was no France. Within a year, Blitzkrieg had finally met its match. Many factors contributed to the German downfall. Not only the dogged spirit of the Soviet armed forces hampered the advance, but also the sub-zero winter that was preceded and followed by *rasputsa*, a period of rain and thaw that turned road and countryside into a morass and caused supply trucks to bog down. In October 1941 alone, 6000 supply trucks on the Smolensk–Vyazma highway had become trapped in a sea of mud. At the same time, the first snows had begun to fall and the Germans on the Eastern Front began to realise how poorly prepared they were for what was to follow. General von Greiffenburg, chief of staff, Twelfth Army, described how weather conditions in the Soviet Union 'make things impassable in the mud of spring and autumn, unbearable in the heat of summer and impossible in the depths of winter. Climate in Russia is a series of natural disasters.'

In the north and the centre it could often reach 40 degrees below freezing in the middle of winter. These temperatures could make the metal of a machine pistol so brittle that the firing pin could easily snap. Another major problem was that the low temperatures would freeze the lubricants and grease inside the guns causing them to completely seize. Not expecting such severe weather, the Germans had not developed any low-temperature gun lubricants, so soldiers had to resort to ad hoc solutions. The most common was to remove all trace of oil and grease, then coat the action with a very fine powder such as flowers of sulphur. In southern Russia, where the climate was less severe, sunflower seed oil provided the answer and replaced the standard gun oil.

Russia's geography also played its part in defeating Germany. The south has arid steppes and sandy wastelands. Broad marshes and forest dominate the central area. To the north there is more forest, permeated with swamps. These forests, primeval swamps and marshes made the manoeuvre warfare that the largely road-bound Germans had employed so successfully in the rest of Europe ineffective. German tactics dictated that the panzers bypassed the forests and swamps to seek out the Russians on open ground. However, the Russians had other ideas, and would retire into the forests and swamps either to turn them into fortresses or to disappear into their depths only to emerge later, far behind the German front line. Unlike the Germans, who would dig in on the edge of a wood, the Russians would move deep inside, digging trenches and clearing undergrowth up to waist height to create low-level all-round fields of fire that were almost impossible to spot. Particular attention was paid to the enemy's rear, where the Soviets could attack from behind any unsuspecting troops that passed through their position. The German army had no experience of fighting in these conditions, where armour, air support and artillery were ineffective. Even the machine gun was of limited use in the dense forests. Here they would have to rely on the machine pistol, rifle and grenade, with heavy mortars as their only support.

The Germans discovered that it was the mountain divisions that were proving to be the most effective units for fighting in these dense forests and swamps. Accordingly, they raised divisions of light infantry and improvised brigades, where the machine pistol was the prime weapon. One such brigade was *Kavallerie Brigade zbV beim Armeeober-kommmando 9*, otherwise known as *Kavallerie Brigade* Model. During the winter of 1941/42, 60,000 Russians had penetrated the rear areas of the General Model's German Ninth Army in large-scale infiltrations of small units - the 'ant strategy' (a term coined by the British military theorist Basil Liddell Hart) as it is often known. Here in the swampy forests close to the River Volga, between Karpov in the north and Vyazma in the south, they forced the Germans to fight on two fronts, threatening supply lines. In July 1942, Model ordered the creation of a special cavalry brigade to neutralise the threat.

ANTI-PARTISAN ACTION

Model formed the brigade out of the reconnaissance battalions from each of the eight divisions under his control and placed it under the command of Colonel Karl-Freidrich von der Meden. The brigade was organised into three cavalry regiments. Cavalry Regiments 1 and 3 had two bicycle squadrons, one cavalry squadron and one heavy squadron. Regiment 2 was organised in the same way, except that it had an additional cavalry squadron. Each squadron was divided into 12 squads of 10 men each, apart from the MG section. Wherever possible the men were equipped with machine pistols. The mounted troops kept their German horses. However, to carry the ammunition, food and baggage, each bicycle squadron was assigned two local horse-drawn Panji wagons. This meant that the whole brigade could keep moving in any terrain. After six weeks training, the brigade formed up south of Olenio along the Luchesa River, ready to move southwards for Operation Seydlitz.

For several days prior to the attack, reconnaissance identified all the positions and trees were cut down to form a corduroy road to the jumping-off point. The attack started at 0300 hours on 2 July. The cavalry swept out of a heavy fog through the surprised Russian first and second lines, taking many prisoners. At noon they turned west to attack the main road through the area, which was heavily defended with antitank positions and obstacles. One regiment crossed through the centre of the dense forest swamps to attack these

positions from the rear and again surprise the Russians. By nightfall a large proportion of the road was under German control, allowing the armour to move forwards. By noon the next day the Russian Thirty-Ninth Army was in full retreat. At its end, Operation Seydlitz had accounted for 50,000 prisoners and had captured 230 tanks and 760 artillery pieces as well as thousands of small arms. In his summing up of the operation, on two separate occasions, Colonel von der Meden stressed the importance of equipping men with machine pistols wherever possible.

Although it was the MP38 and MP40 that were supplied to the troops on all sectors of the Eastern Front, troops made great use of captured Russian or even Finnish machine pistols in addition to their own weapons. They preferred them because of their considerably higher magazine capacity and greater reliability in the abhorrent weather conditions. *SS-Untersturmführer* Erich Heller of *Das Reich* SS Panzer Division described his own weapons as he moved to the Russian front line in August 1942: 'I armed myself well. I had my pistol, my rifle and also a wonderful Finnish machine pistol, a superb weapon. I also had some egg grenades and stick grenades - stowed away so that they could not be hit by any stray bullets. I was a travelling arsenal.'

STREET FIGHTING

At the battle for Stalingrad, every square inch of ground was fiercely contested. The Russian defence was based on centres of resistance, which were normally groups of heavily fortified houses interconnected by trenches or sewer systems. Here a single house could be manned by as little as a section or up to a whole company, depending on its importance. Amongst the rubble and ruins, the Germans forfeited their superiority in mobile tactics. Panzers, with their restricted movement, were picked off in the streets, one by one, by the tenacious Russian infantry. German troops would normally assault buildings by day, where possible with armour in support. Taking a leaf from the Germans' tactical manuals, the Russians formed storm groups consisting of an assault group, reinforcements and a reserve. Their task was to break in to a building and wage an independent, miniature battle

Left: A German squad house-clearing in the Soviet Union, their machine pistols and rifle held at the ready. The MP40 was ideally suited for such close range work.

Below: Don Cossacks being briefed by a Soviet officer north of Stalingrad. The MP40 was a popular weapon amongst the Cossacks – here the patrol commander wears his in the German style.

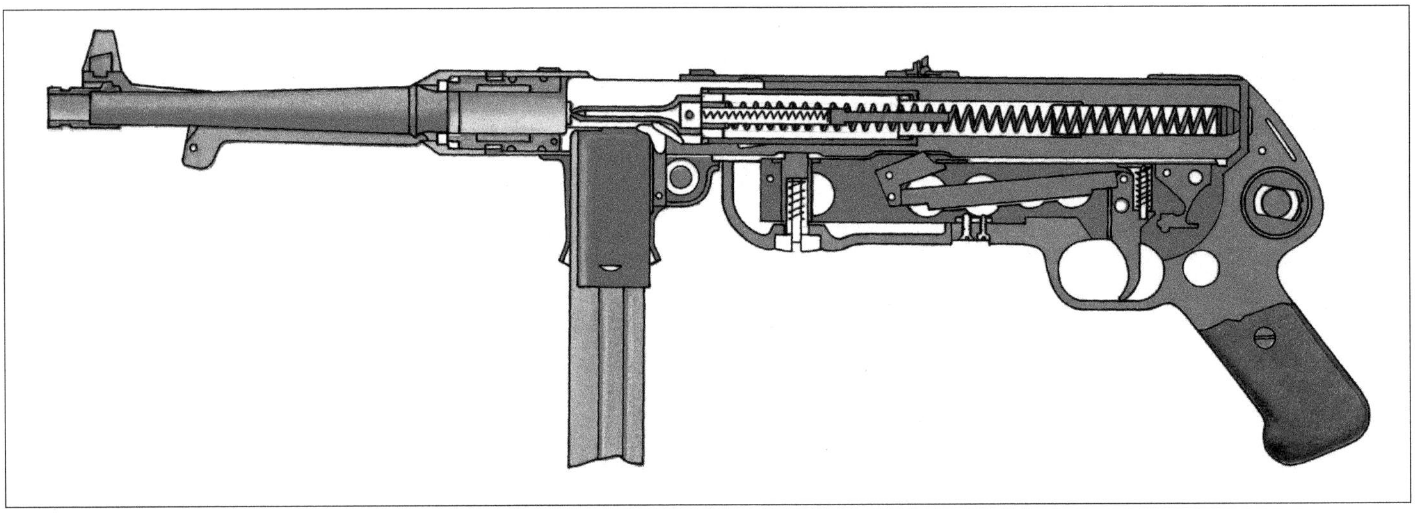

inside. These attacks were timed according to the Germans' sleeping and eating habits as well as changes in watch, and almost always launched at night or under the cover of massive smoke screens. Horrifyingly savage battles took place, where the front lines could be different rooms in the same building. In these conditions even the rifle had limited effectiveness. Instead, the main weapons on both sides were machine pistols, grenades, flame-throwers and pistols. They also returned to an almost medieval style of warfare using spades with razor sharp edges and daggers. Here the advantages of the machine pistol were repeatedly demonstrated. They were easily carried and did not require much space to fire. Also in these conditions, they did not require accurate aiming and could deliver a devastating amount of firepower. The major drawback of the MP38 and MP40, their limited magazine capacity, became more apparent as well. In close-quarter firefights, where the distance between opponents could be measured in feet, the magazine could be emptied in moments, and before the operator had time to change it, the Russians would be upon him. It was this shortcoming that prompted the development of the MP40II with its twin magazine.

Left: Cutaway of the MP38, clearly showing how the main spring is protected from foreign objects like mud and stones by the telescopic tube in which it is housed.

Another type of street fighting where machine pistols played an important part was demonstrated by Battle Group Scherer. After the German retreat from Moscow, the Russian Third Shock Army began to advance on the strategically important town of Cholm, which was surrounded by impenetrable marsh. Here was the only bridge across the marsh and a major junction of north-south and east-west roads. In the little town was a mixture of the remnants of two infantry divisions, a Luftwaffe field regiment plus a few police and several navy drivers altogether totalling just 3500 men. By the 21 January they were completely cut off and for many days resisted repeated attacks by the Red Army round the 2km perimeter. Then on 23 February (Red Army Day), the Soviets launched a major offensive against the town. The attacking armour was soon brought to a halt by tank-hunting teams and the Germans' one and only PAK gun. On the eastern side of the town, the Russian troops charged down the narrow streets shoulder to shoulder and so tightly packed that those at the front were pushed along by those behind. At the opposite end of each street the Germans set up two or three MG34s, which tore the solid masses of advancing men apart.

Despite the carnage, the Russians still pressed forwards. Eventually, with such a huge number of men attacking them, the German gunners were forced to withdraw. As they pulled back, German reserves armed with machine pistols and machine guns stepped into their place. After pouring hand and rifle grenades into the Soviet front ranks, the reserves began to march up the street in short lines. It was like the slaughter of the French columns at Waterloo. In the crush of men, those behind the front ranks could not bring their weapons to bear. Under an unwavering hail of automatic fire, the surviving Soviets eventually turned tail and ran back the way they came. Altogether, the beleaguered Germans held out against more than 100 separate assaults from six infantry divisions, six independent brigades and two tank brigades before the siege was lifted, after 105 days and nights. Relief came in the form of an attack by the 411 Infantry Regiment, a number of tanks and a self-propelled gun group, supported by Stukas.

Left: Panzergrenadiers disembark from a Sdkfz 250/1. The standard gruppe was ten men commanded by a gruppenführer armed with a machine pistol. A second machine pistol was carried on the Sdkfz 250/1.

Left: A sergeant in the SS Wiking Division seen in early 1944. Along with his MP40 he is wearing thick winter clothing with a fleece-lined hood in an attempt to keep out the Russian cold.

During World War II, the machine pistol really came into its own when it was deployed for the purpose from which the original concept first arose: assaulting defensive fortifications. A prime example of this is the attack by a paratroop assault battalion capturing a ridge, held by a reinforced Russian battalion, that connected two hills. Led by mine clearing teams and supported by flame-thrower detachments, the German assault companies advanced in total silence. Suddenly, two mines exploded in quick succession. The advantage of surprise now lost, the battalion had to make a rapid frontal assault against the entrenched Russians before they had time to react to the explosions.

James Lucas, in his book *Storming Eagles*, describes what happened next:

The Engineer group leader orders 'Flame!' and a sheet of fire envelopes the first Russian strong-point in the outpost line. Machine-pistol fire pours into the bunker which erupts in a loud explosion. In addition to the sentries on duty it must have held explosive charges or mines. That's one strong-point dealt with and all along the battalion front other bunkers fall to the Para's swift advance. The charge moves across the unmanned first trench line and into a shallow wadi where the Ivans are sleeping in their dug-outs. Red Army men awakened by the sound of firing start to pour out of the dug-outs but before they can grasp what is happening bullets from the machine-pistols cut them down. Flame-throwers are in action all along the line and then the heavy detonations of satchel charges as these blow up one bunker after another. The Jaeger work their way along the second line of Russian trenches, bombing and machine-pistolling their way forward, rolling up the enemy line. Suddenly, there are no Ivans left. Those that have not been killed or taken prisoner have fled. The objective has been taken. Soon the first groups from the Jaeger battalions come up to relieve the assault battalion and to consolidate the area. The attack has been a success.

THE WESTERN FRONT 1944–45

By the time of the battle for Normandy, the Allies had total superiority in the air. This meant that, for fear of air attack, the large convoys of German supply vehicles that had been characteristic of earlier campaigns were impossible. It also meant that the infantry had only limited – if any – air support for their attacks. Despite their failures in the East, a great deal of emphasis was still placed on infiltration and small-group actions. Storm battalions were used as spearheads for counterattacks. Groups, sometimes as small as two or three men, often armed only with machine pistols and a Teller

antitank mine, would find the gaps in the Allies' lines and penetrate far behind them.

Weight of fire was still considered critical to success and the small-group action was a building block for a larger offensive. A Canadian battle report from 1944 described the German fighting methods:

> *Experience has shown that the Germans will almost invariably launch a counter-attack to break up an attack by small infantry units. You can expect such a counter-attack, usually by 10 to 20 men, not more than five minutes after you get close to the German positions. They are usually well armed with light machine guns and machine pistols, and counter attack by fire and movement. They keep up heavy fire while small details, even individuals, alternately push forward. The Germans almost always attack your flank. They seldom close with bayonet, but try to drive you out by fire.*

Above: This view shows the hollow shoulder pad of the MP40. The stock would usually be extended even if firing from the hip, so that an elbow could pin it to the body and help stabilise the gun.

An example of this type of defence came during the fighting around Falaise during late summer 1944. The 12th SS Panzer Division *Hitler Jugend* had moved into Normandy only two months before D-Day, taking up a line between Alençon and Crelouges. By August, along with thousands of other troops, they had been squeezed into a pocket centred on Falaise, the main rail and communication centre for the

Above: Captured in large quantities by both Americans and Russians, MP40s were found in many countries' arsenals after the war, including Israeli paratroops (above), Norwegian tank crews and the Viet Cong.

area. It was essential that the town be held as long as possible to allow as many troops as possible time to escape the pocket. This task was given to just 200 men – the remnants of the 1st Battalion of the 26th Panzer Grenadier Regiment – along with two Tiger tanks from the 102nd Panzer Battalion. Opposing them was an entire Canadian infantry brigade supported by two squadrons of Sherman tanks. Inevitably, facing so few defenders, the Canadians broke through the perimeter on the right flank and headed for the town centre. When the German commander, *Sturmbannführer* Krause heard the news, he immediately counterattacked with 20 men from the HQ. With Krause at their head, the Germans charged the Canadians, throwing hand grenades and firing machine pistols, then engaging them in vicious hand to hand combat with entrenching tools and bayonets. Eventually, they repulsed the attack. However, this only postponed the inevitable. Slowly, the Canadians tightened their stranglehold around the town. The Germans inside put up a fanatical resistance. Small groups of men determined to fight to the last counterattacked time and time again, firing their machine pistols as they charged the Canadians. Soon, against such overwhelming opposition, the Germans held only the school house of the Abbey of St Jean Baptiste, and then this too was reduced to rubble and flames. By late August, the pocket had closed. The thousands of Germans still inside trying to flee northwards towards the River Seine were trapped inside. However, the heroic last stand by elements of *Hitler Jugend* allowed thousands more to escape and fight again.

In Europe, away from the frozen wastes of Russia, the MP40 was far more reliable. It was nicknamed the 'Burp gun' by the GIs, for whom the MP40 was a prized possession, which they frequently preferred to their own weapons. Because of its distinctive sound, Allied users of the MP40 invited all manner of return fire, especially at night. So, to stop themselves being targeted by friendly fire, it was not uncommon for US troops with captured weapons to chop two inches from the return spring, thus changing the sound (as well as the rate of fire).

THE WEREWOLVES

By September 1944 the Allies were closing on Berlin. In a last-ditch attempt to stave off inevitable defeat and force a stalemate, Hitler and the remnants of the Nazi party tried to incite a massed insurrection against the Allies by the people. As part of this uprising a partisan army was formed from the young and old to operate behind the Allied lines called

Werwolf (Werewolf). Training for this secret organisation was already underway in the late spring of 1944. By the end of the war over 5000 had passed through the five-week training course. After learning how to use weapons, explosives and communications as well as survival methods, they returned to their homes to await orders. Secret supply dumps were set up to equip the werewolves when the time came. Because they were easy to conceal and because of the rate of fire, most of these partisans were equipped with machine pistols. As the war came to an end they carried out many operations in both eastern and western Europe, although most had little impact. A radio proclamation by Goebbels, attempting to induce an open revolt, not only for the first time publicly admitted the existence of such an organisation, but also changed the Werewolves from a proper partisan organisation to a disorganised rabble where anyone with a weapon could attack any foreigner. The proclamation had the opposite effect to what had been intended. If the Werewolves had been directly controlled, then perhaps they might have had more of an impact. Instead, when Hitler committed suicide, most resistance died with him.

THE MP38 AND MP40 AFTER WORLD WAR II

Many German weapons factories and their undelivered stock were captured by the Allies during the closing stages of World War II. Countries in the west that had been overrun by the Germans and occupied needed to rearm. With so many surplus MP40s available for redistribution, substantial numbers were given to the Netherlands and Norway in particular. They later armed their tank crews with them, where they remained in service until the mid-1980s. France, too, equipped some of its troops with the MP40 before French alternatives became available.

The Russians distributed their captured MP40s as military aid to emerging communist states such as Cuba and several southern and central American countries. MP40s were also used in the Greek Civil War (1946–49) and the Arab–Israeli war of 1948–49. They even appeared in Vietnam in the hands of Viet Cong guerrillas. Nowadays, however, they are most likely to be seen in the hands of collectors or enthusiasts.

Below: Former Greek Communist guerrillas pose for the camera armed with a variety of weapons from World War II, including an MP40, an M1A1, a Bren gun and a mortar.

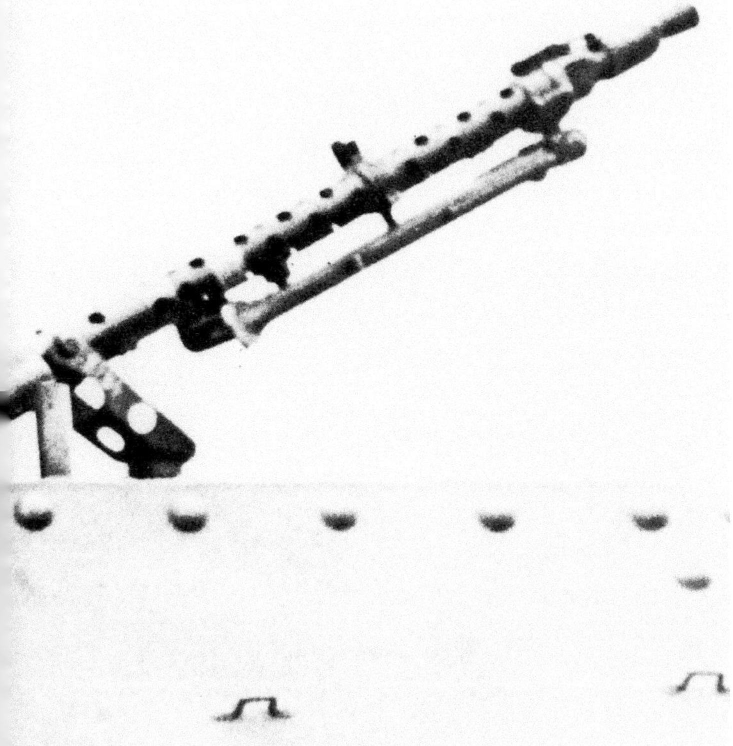

CHAPTER 6

Other Machine Pistols of World War II

During the later months of the war, there came a need to arm the local defence (*Volksturm*) forces that had been set up to defend the German homeland. One weapon was the Volksmaschinen-pistole MP3008 or Gerät Neumünster. It was little more than the British Sten gun with a vertical magazine.

Captured Stens had been in use by the German occupation forces in France for several years. They had renamed it the 9mm MP749(e). The MP3008 was even cruder than the original, made not in major factories but small workshops all over the country. The speedy collapse of the Third Reich meant that no more than 5000 were built.

These were not the only Stens to be built by the Germans. As part of a top secret project, 25,000 exact Sten Mk IIs, even with British markings, were built over six weeks in late 1944 by the Mauser Werke at Oberndorf. The weapon was known as the Potsdam instrument (*Gerät Potsdam*). Although their purpose was never identified, at a cost of RM1800 per gun it must have been of great importance. No one knows what happened to them after they left the factory.

OTHER GERMAN MACHINE PISTOLS

With the MP40 already in production at his factory, C.G. Haenel in Suhl, Hugo Schmeisser began to develop a new machine pistol of his own. In 1941 he unveiled the MP41, which combined the stock and fire selector of his MP28 with the barrel, receiver and magazine of the MP40. He also used the MP40's telescopic spring tube. The only new feature was the rigid attachment of the body to the wooden stock. This meant that in order to remove the breech, the cap at the rear of the body - held by a spring clip - had to be pulled off. Very

Left: A Waffen-SS artilleryman fires a captured Russian PPSh 41 submachine gun. The PPSh 41 was much prized, as it was extremely robust, needed little maintenance and had a 71-round magazine.

few MP41s were ever built, because Schmeisser was taken to court after he infringed Vollmer's patent by using the latter's telescopic tube in the design. The project was cancelled.

Another development from ERMA was the EMP44. This design was simplicity itself, with the barrel casing, body and buttstock made from a single straight tube, with a pistol grip and shoulder piece made from the same tube and welded on at right angles. The shoulder piece also doubled as the end closure for the body. The double side by side magazine of the MP40II was used with separate catches, and the tubular muzzle brake and compensator were welded on. Although prototypes were built, the MP44 never reached production.

THE THOMPSON

By 1928, after an intense marketing campaign, Thompson had managed to secure a small order of his sub-machine guns from the US Marines for their expeditionary force in Nicaragua. The US Cavalry followed suit soon after, and ordered 400 for the crews of its armoured vehicles, calling it the M1928A1. A more substantial order followed in 1939, this time from the French, who ordered 3750 Model 1928s.

Although the idea of a machine pistol had previously been rejected by Britain's armed forces, a complete reversal in attitude came late in December 1939. The British Expeditionary Force (BEF) in France sent a request to the Ordnance Board (OB) for the immediate supply of machine carbines (as machine pistols were then called in Britain, when they were not called 'gangster guns'). The OB preferred the Finnish machine pistol and had reservations regarding the cost and quality of the Thompson sub-machine gun. However, because of its availability, the Thompson was chosen to meet the immediate needs of the army. After the BEF was evacuated from Dunkirk, there was the threat of an imminent invasion from Germany and a huge shortage of weaponry. The British Army asked Auto Ordnance initially to supply 450 weapons but by the end of 1940 this had risen to 107,500. The US Government by this time had ordered a further 20,450.

These were supplied as the M1928A2 and were essentially Model 1921s. However, unlike the previous model, it had a straight below the barrel hand grip in place of the front pistol grip. The buttstock was fixed, and in place of the drum magazine a 30-round box was introduced. Previously only available as an option on the 1928 model, the Cutts' Compensator was also added as standard. This device was invented by a retired US Marines Colonel, Richard M. Cutts, and his son, Richard M. Cutts Jnr, also an officer in the Marines. The Cutts' Compensator fitted to the end of the barrel and had four slots in the top that forced the gases upwards, which in turn kept the muzzle from rising and improved the accuracy.

As the war progressed some of the earlier refinements were taken off to speed up production. The Lyman rear sight was removed and changed to a simple open sight with two wings to protect it. The Hesitation Lock was omitted, as was the Cutts' Compensator. The design was finally fixed on 25 April 1942 as the SMG Cal .45 M1. A further modification in October saw the firing pin machined into face, changing the model designation to M1A1. These refinements drastically

Below: An M1928 AC Thompson submachine gun with a Cutts Compensator attached to the end of the muzzle. In theory this forced the waste gases out of the slots in the top, reducing muzzle climb.

reduced the cost of each gun from $209 for a 1939 M1928 to $44.50 for a 1944 M1A1, and it came complete with magazine spares and a cleaning kit! At the height of production, 90,000 guns were being manufactured each month, and when, in 1944, production ended, a total of 1,383,043 of the three main versions had been built.

The Royal Navy and the Royal Air Force were also both desperate for new weapons after Dunkirk, the latter for the defence of its airfields. The demand for Thompson submachine guns was already outstripping supply, so it was decided to build a copy of Schmeisser's MP28. Made by the Stirling Armament Company in Dagenham, it was to become known as the Lanchester Mk 1, after its designer George Herbert Lanchester. It was almost identical to the MP28 II, the only differences being that the fire selector was located in front of the trigger guard instead of above it, the release button to break it for stripping was larger, and it had a mount for the long British bayonet. Like the German weapons of 10 years earlier, it was made to the highest standards and of the finest materials, including a solid brass magazine housing and a 50-round stick magazine. Also, like the MP28, it fired a 9mm Parabellum cartridge, originally German, later from Winchester in the US. The order for 50,000 Lanchesters was delivered exclusively to the Royal Navy in 1941.

Above: British commandos armed with the M1928 AC Thompson. The commandos were the first British unit to use the Thompson in anger on their various raids against occupied Europe.

THE STEN GUN

In January 1941 it was announced that a new, greatly simplified machine pistol had been developed. Its name was

Above: The M1A1 version of the Thompson, without the Cutts Compensator and with a wooden foregrip, seen carried by a US paratrooper as he boards a C-47 Dakota before D-Day.

taken from the initials of the officer in charge of the Small Arms Group, Major R.V. Shepherd, a director of BSA, and its designer H.J. Turpin. To this the first two letters of Enfield were added and Britains most famous machine pistol of World War II, the Sten, was born. The troops themselves had little regard for it, calling it the 'Woolworth special', after the mass-market chain store, or the 'plumbers delight'.

The first model, the 9mm Sten Mk1, was like the MP40 in that it was designed to be as cheap and quick to produce as possible. Also, as with the MP40, many sub-assemblies were made all over the country and brought to Royal Ordnance and BSA factories for assembly. It was a very crude weapon, the body being no more than a steel tube with a steel framework for the butt. Protruding horizontally from the left-hand side was the magazine housing which held a 32-round single-feed box magazine. A steel tube also served as the hand grip, and it had a wooden stock to house the trigger mechanism. Other

Right: A British infantryman carrying a Sten Mk II. It was a simple blowback weapon, firing from an open bolt, with a handle in a slot on the receiver cocking the weapon.

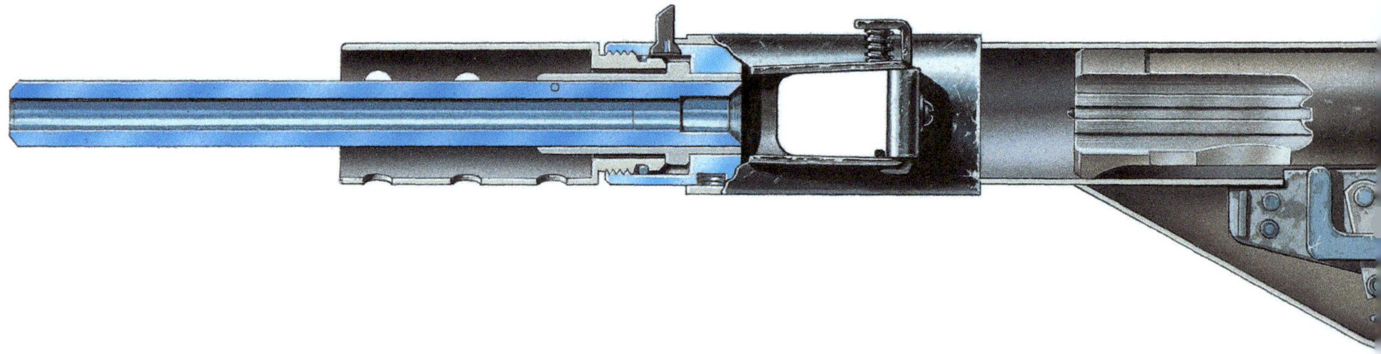

Calibre	9mm
Length	762mm (30in)
Weight	3.7kg (8.16lb)
Feed	32-round box magazine
System of operation	blowback
Rate of fire (cyclic)	550rpm
Muzzle velocity	365mps (1200ft/s)

9mm Sten Mk II

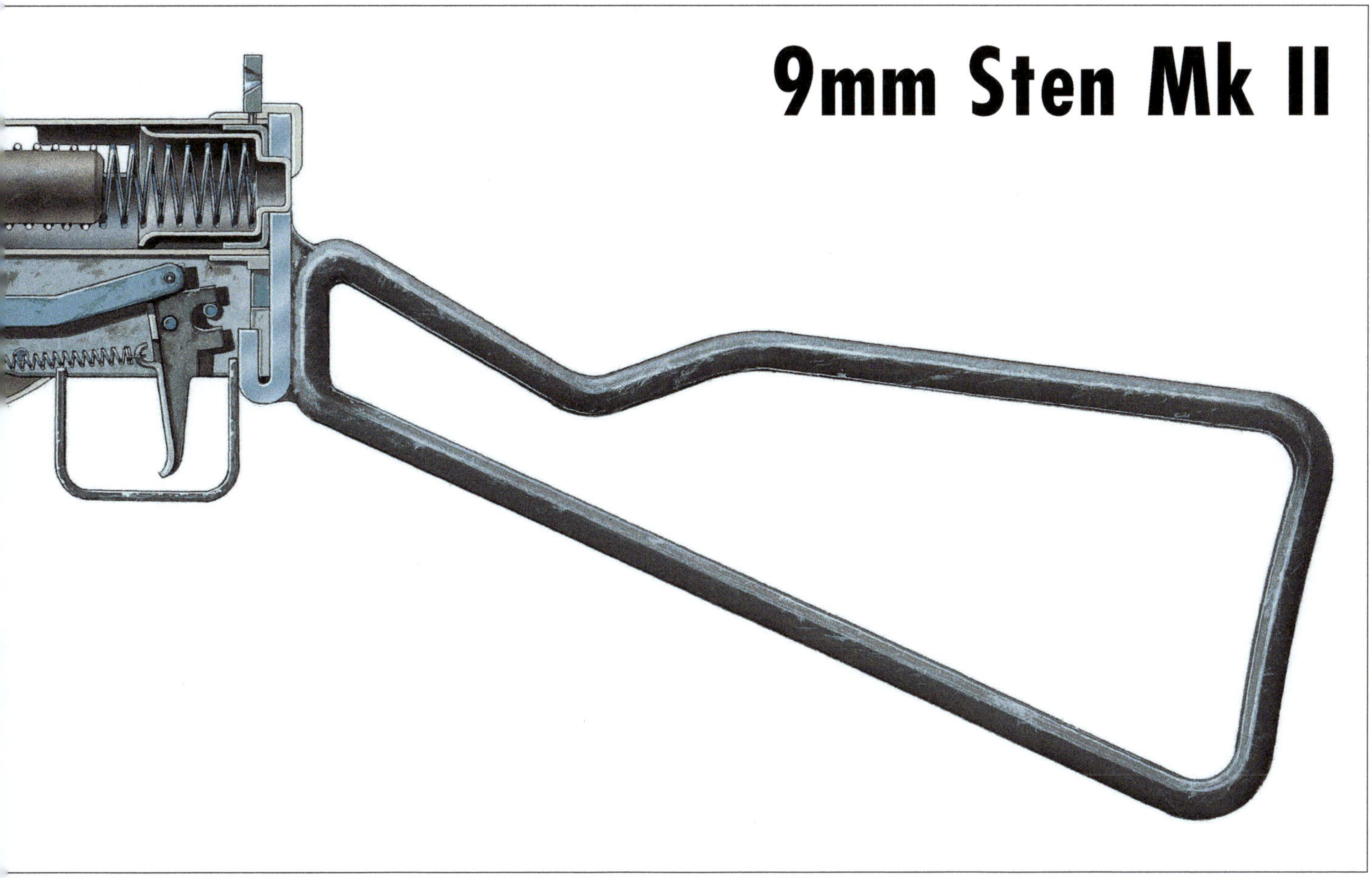

Left: Easily broken down and concealed, the Sten Mk II became a favourite with resistance and partisan forces across Europe, such as the Italians pictured. Many were delivered by parachute container.

than this, the only machined parts were in the operating mechanism, the bolt being a basic cylinder with a fixed firing pin. The action was simple blowback that fired from an open bolt. A handle operating in a slot in the receiver cocked the weapon. This slot had a notch towards the rear into which the handle could be pushed to act as a safety. The Sten had a cyclic rate of around 600rpm on automatic and could be changed to single shot by a push-through selector. Within months, 100,000 had been delivered before production switched to an even simpler Mk II.

More than two million Sten Mk IIs were built, and it is now regarded as the classic model despite there being nine other variants. It had a butt made from a single tube with a cross-bar welded on for the shoulder piece. The wooden stock was replaced with a sheet-metal box. The magazine housing was also redesigned to allow it to be rotated downwards once the magazine had been removed, protecting the innards of the gun from dirt. The Sten could be broken down very easily to allow it to be maintained. This meant that in the hands of resistance and partisan forces in occupied Europe, to whom tens of thousands were delivered by parachute, it could be easily hidden.

SOVIET MACHINE PISTOLS

During 1940 the Soviet Union had been at war with the Finns. Here the machine pistol had been employed in large numbers by both sides, and had proved particularly effective for the close-quarter fighting that frequently took place. The main Russian machine pistol at the time was the PPD40, an upgraded PPD34/38, with an improved bolt and a floating firing pin that was controlled by a lever in the bolt. However, like the German weapons of the generation before, it was time-consuming to produce. Development of a replacement was already underway when Hitler invaded the Soviet Union in June 1941. Designed by Georgiy S. Shpagin, it was to be known as the PPSh41. Production began in 1942 and by the time the war ended more than five million had been built.

Like its German counterpart, the MP40, it was quick and cheap to produce, with a pressed barrel jacket and receiver that was hinged at the front end of the wooden forestock. This made field stripping very easy. Pressing the receiver catch forwards allowed the barrel to be tipped up. The return spring and bolt could then be withdrawn.

Considering it was mass-produced, the PPSh41was extremely robust. It had a conventional blowback operating system and selective fire, firing 900rpm on full automatic. A buffer of laminated leather or felt blocks was used to absorb the shock of the breech as it recoiled. Like its predecessor it had a chromed barrel, the jacket of which extended past

Above: The Sten Mk V, seen here on the left, entered service in 1944 and was a refined version of the Sten with several improvements including a wooden stock.

the end of the muzzle and sloped back from top to bottom. In the top of the extension was a gas-exit port that acted as a rudimentary compensator to keep the muzzle down at full auto. The PPSh41 was chambered for the 7.23mm M1930 cartridge. The magazine was either a 71-round drum or a 35-round box that was slightly curved. To fill the drum, the cover first had to be removed by pressing a button at the rear which released the catch on the front. Once open, the spring had to be turned two complete turns anti-clockwise. The cartridge conveyor had to be held still for the first complete revolution. The spiral track insert then had to be turned anti-clockwise as far as possible; 71 rounds could then be inserted into the track nose-up. When it was fully loaded, the rotor was turned anti-clockwise against the spring. Finally, the central button was pressed while the rotor was turned clockwise until it stopped. The cover could then be replaced and locked into position.

Even simpler was the PPS42. This was born out of the desperation that ensued during the German siege of Leningrad in 1942. Completely surrounded, the Russians were in desperate need of weapons, so A.I. Sudarev designed a weapon that could be built quickly in the many machine shops that dotted the city. It was made entirely from sheet steel, stamped into shape, riveted and spot-welded together. It had a cyclic rate of 650rpm that was fed from a 35-round box magazine. To trial the weapon, it was simply taken off the production line and into the field, its performance reported back and the appropriate changes made on the line.

DEPENDABLE WEAPONS

In the field, whole battalions and regiments would be equipped with the PPSh41. Shock assault units riding into battle on the back of T34 tanks frequently only carried machine pistols and hand grenades. Under the harsh conditions of the Eastern Front they often received no maintenance or cleaning, yet in the hands of the Russians who swept across Eastern Russia and Europe by the thousand, the PPSh41 proved dependable and reliable.

THE M3 GREASE GUN

By the beginning of 1941 the US army, after observing Stens and MP40s in Europe, acknowledged the important role machine pistols had to play on the battlefield. With the expensive Thompson already in production, the US Army Ordnance Board initiated a study to develop their own Sten type weapon in October 1942. The requirement for the new weapon was that it was to be of all-metal construction, easily broken down and with a cost and performance equal to the Sten. It should also fire either the .45 APC or 9mm round with the minimum of conversion. The task of designing the new weapon was given to George Hyde of the Inland Division of General Motors. Prototypes were ready by November, and in December the weapon was officially adopted as the M3. The same tests that scrutinised the MP40 were applied to the M3. In the endurance tests it only had two malfunctions in 5000 rounds and scored 95 out of 100.

The M3 was constructed from sheet-metal stampings with only the barrel, breech and firing mechanism machined. The main body was essentially two 365.8mm (14.4in) metal halves welded together to form a cylinder. On the front end was a knurled cap, into the centre of which was screwed the 20cm (8in) barrel. Projecting down from the rear of the tube was a metal pistol grip, while projecting backwards was a tubular-steel telescopic butt that retracted into tubes either side of the body in the middle. In fact it looked just like its nickname, the 'grease gun'. On the right-hand side of the trigger casing, just forward and above the trigger

Below: Unlike other combatants in World War II, the Soviets issued whole battalions with submachine guns such as the PPSh 41 shown below, who would ride into battle on tanks.

was the flimsy cocking handle. The whole mechanism had nine components. On the top of the tube was the hinged ejection slot cover, which - when closed with the bolt retracted - acted as the safety, a projection from the casing into the body that prevented the bolt from moving. The bolt was drilled longitudinally to take a pair of guide rods around which were the twin return springs. This meant that the machining tolerances of the bolt were not so critical.

THE M3A1

Production was carried out by the Guide Lamp Division of General Motors in Indiana. Later the bolts were also made at the Buffalo Arms Co and the Rock Island Arsenal. Several other variants of the gun were also built including the M3A1. On this, the complicated cocking mechanism was removed, a recess machined into the breech and the ejection port extended to enable the full breech-block travel to be exposed. This meant that to cock the gun, the firer simply opened the cover, placed his finger into the recess and pulled the breech back. By war's end a total of 606,694 M3s and M3A1s had been built.

Left: PPSh 41s were widely available on the battlefield, as was their ammunition, and as a consequence German troops like the Waffen-SS at Kursk shown could use them with little difficulty.

Above: In Stalingrad whole companies fought for control of a single house. In the foreground is a PPSh 41; directly behind is a captured MP40. The man at the window has just been shot.

After his work on the Modello 1918 and two self-loading carbines, Marengoni was promoted to head of Research and Development at Beretta and continued his work on machine pistols. Here he developed a completely new machine pistol, more complex than its predecessors yet far more reliable. It was known as the Modello 1938 and would become the Italian army's standard machine pistol until 1960.

BERETTA'S SUBMACHINE GUN

Unlike its contemporaries, every Modello 1938 was hand-crafted. This showed in combat, as it proved accurate and reliable under all conditions. It had a wooden stock, a tubular body, jacketed barrel and a magazine mounted vertically downwards. The trigger mechanism was similar to the one Marengoni used on the modified Villar Perosa, in that it had two triggers, the forward one for single-shot and the rear one for automatic. It operated by simple blowback, with no retarding mechanism. When the bolt had moved fully forwards, a cam came in to contact the ejector stud. It was revolved to drive the firing pin fully forwards. The rear of the small-diameter return spring was mounted in a tube in the end of the body's end cap, while the other end sat over a guide tube extending out from the bolt, bearing on the firing pin. Initially, the Modello 1938A, as the first model was called, was chambered to fire the high-powered 9x19mm M38 round, although this was later changed to the standard 9mm Parabellum. Several different sizes of box magazine, holding either 10, 20, 30 or 40 rounds, were issued with the weapon.

Three other versions of the basic design were developed: the first was the Modello 1, designed in 1941 for airborne troops. It was of all-metal construction, with a fixed firing pin, a shorter barrel (without cooling jacket) and a 40-round box magazine in the forward hand grip. Like the German MP38, it had a foldable tubular stock, while the pistol grip, trigger guard and housing were all made from aluminium.

The second, the Modello M38/42, was a simplified version of the 1938A and was the first Italian model to be mass-produced. The body was the same as the Modello 1, except it had a short wooden buttstock and a wooden forestock that ended at the magazine housing. Unlike its predecessor, it had a magazine housing with no provision for a hand grip.

The third model, an even simpler version of the M38/42, was known as the M1938/44. It had a smaller bolt and an enlarged return spring (similar to the Sten). The only external difference between the two models was that the small projection in the centre of the rear cap that housed the return-spring rod was missing from the later version.

When Italy changed sides in 1943, the Germans seized all available weapons and production resources from the Italians, including many M38/42s, which were turned against the Allies as the MP738(i). Under German supervision, Beretta manufactured a further 231,193 of the weapons before the Gardone factory was finally captured by the Allies in 1945.

THE ZK 383

Several European machine pistols and their production lines were captured by the Germans in 1940 and pressed into service. When they occupied Czechoslovakia in 1939, the SS took over the Brno Weapons factory, including the production lines for the Zbrojovka Koucky (ZK) 383. This had been designed in 1933 by Josef and Fratisek Koucky and was also the standard for the Bulgarian army. Manufactured to a high standards, it had an integral folding bipod and the unusual feature of two rates of fire. These were controlled by adding a 170g (6oz) weight to the bolt to reduce it from 700 to 500rpm. It was adopted by the Germans as the MP383, and all wartime production models were given to the SS, primarily on the Eastern Front.

Right: A demonstration in the desert for visiting top brass. Two captured weapons are shown: the MP40, and, with only its barrel visible, the Beretta M38, in the hands of the soldier wearing a tam-o'-shanter.

Calibre	7.62mm
Length	828mm (32.6in)
Weight	5.4kg (11.9lb)
Feed	71-round drum or 35-round box
System of operation	blowback
Rate of fire (cyclic)	900rpm
Muzzle velocity	488mps (1600ft/s)

PPSh41

THE MAS 38

With the fall of France came another machine pistol, when the Manufacture d'Armes de Saint-Etienne was captured intact. Here the French manufactured the MAS mle 38. The French had begun development of their own machine pistol in 1935 but is was not until 1939 that the first production models appeared and only then for the security police (*Garde Mobile*). The army was equipped with the Thompson. The MAS mle 38 had two unusual features. First, because of the build-up of kinetic energy caused by the long travel of the bolt, the sear had a spring buffer. Second, it fired a 7.65mm Longue round unique to France. It was because of the rarity of this round that the gun's use during World War II was restricted to the German occupation troops in France (when it was designated as the MP722(f)), to French police forces and to French Commandos.

Above: The MAS 38 was an unusual weapon. Although compact, it was difficult to manufacture, and, crucially, only fired French 7.65mm ammunition, which restricted its sales and later use by the Germans.

Below: The M3 'Grease Gun', the US equivalent of the British Sten. Made largely from sheet-metal stampings, the weapon was cheap to manufacture and reliable, but was not popular with its users.

Glossary

Barrel. The rifled tube that gives spin to the bullet.

Bent. A notch cut into the bolt that enables it to be held by the sear in the ready position.

Blowback operation. An operating system in which the force provided by the firing of the bullet returns the bolt to the firing position.

Body. The part of the machine pistol that contains the bolt and return spring. In front is the barrel, behind is the buffer and end cap.

Bolt. The metal cylinder that takes the round from the magazine, feeds it into the chamber and supports it during firing. It also often houses the firing pin.

Breech block. The bolt.

Buffer. A spring placed at the rear of the body to absorb energy from the return action of the bolt.

Chamber. The rear part of the barrel that holds the cartridge before firing.

Change lever. The lever that allows the firer to select the method of fire - either single shot or fully automatic.

Cocking handle. A projection from the bolt that the firer pulls back to cock the gun.

Delayed blowback operation. A system that uses the friction of the bolt on its track to slow it down on the return stroke, allowing the gases time to escape.

Ejector. A projection in the bolt that strikes the cartridge case, forcing it out of the gun once it has been withdrawn by the extractor.

End cap. The rear end of the body, often removable to facilitate extraction of the working parts.

Extractor. A spring-loaded claw attachment to the bolt which springs over the cartridge case to withdraw it from the chamber.

Fire selector lever. The change lever.

Interrupter. A device that, when engaged, disconnects the sear from the trigger after a single round is fired.

Operating spring. The return spring

Receiver. The body.

Retracting handle. The cocking handle.

Return spring. The helical spring situated behind the bolt. As the bolt moves to the rear it is compressed, storing energy. It is this energy that drives the bolt forwards on pressing the trigger.

Rifling. A series of helical grooves cut into the inside of the barrel that cause the bullet to spin and retain stability in flight, improving accuracy.

Sear. The part of the trigger mechanism that engages in the bent to hold it in position.

The improved squad (Gruppe) (late World War I)

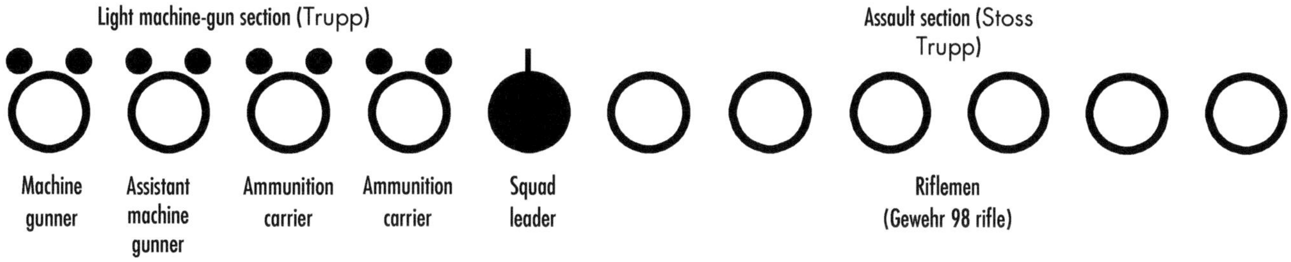

The squad (Gruppe) (early World War II)

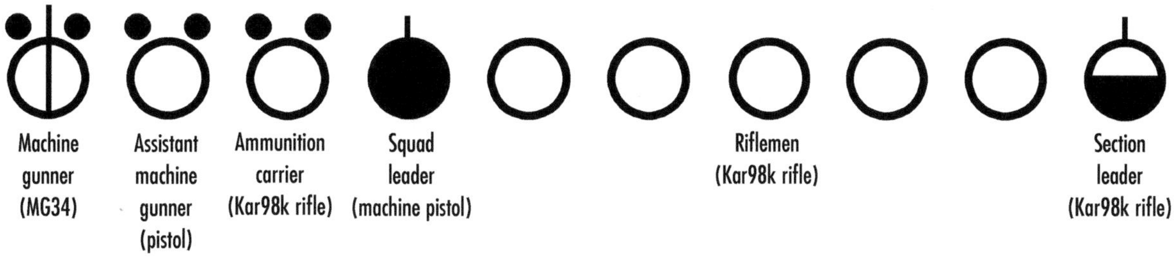

The armoured infantry squad (Panzergrenadiergruppe) (World War II)

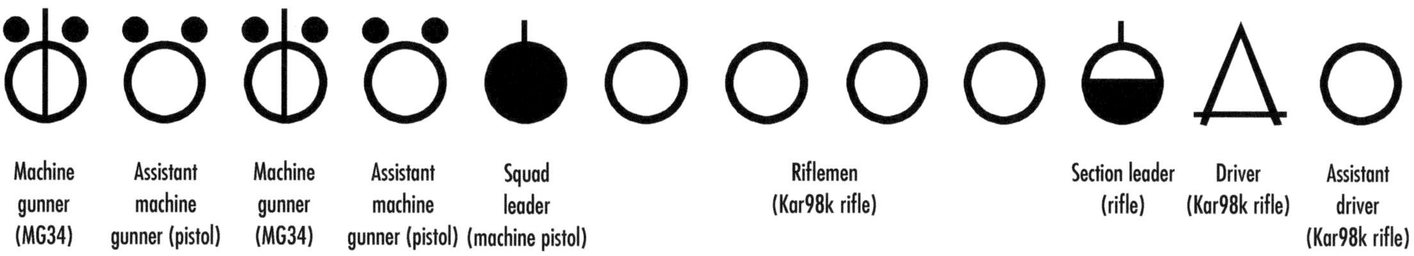

The MP40's Main Rivals

MODEL	MP181	MP2811	ERMA EMP
Country of origin	Germany	Germany	Germany
Manufacturer	Theodore Bergmann Weapons Factory, Suhl	Peiper Weapons Factory, Herstal, Belgium	Erfurt Machine Factory, Berthold Geipel GmbH
Function	Fully automatic with blowback system	Fully automatic with blowback system	Fully automatic with blowback system
Type of fire	Automatic only	Single-shot or sustained	Single-shot or sustained
Overall length	82cm (32in)	82cm (32in)	90.2cm (35.1in)
Barrel length	20cm (7.87in)	20cm (7.87in)	25.1cm (9.9in)
Ammunition	9x19mm Parabellum (08 pistol)	9x19mm Parabellum (08 pistol)	9x19mm Parabellum (08 pistol)
Number of riflings	6	6	6
Rifling direction	Right	Right	Right
Muzzle velocity	381m/s (1269ft/s)	381m/s (1269ft/s)	390m/s (1299ft/s)
Rate of fire, cyclic	350–450 rounds per minute (rpm)	500–600rpm	500rpm
Effective range	70m (230ft)	70m (230ft)	70m (230ft)
Magazine capacity	20 rounds (stick) or 32 rounds (drum)	20 rounds (stick) or 32 rounds (stick)	32 rounds (stick)
Sight	Folding scope with two notches	Folding scope with two notches	Fixed sight with flap for 100–200m (110–220 yards)
Weight, unloaded	4.2kg (9.25lb)	4kg (8.8lb)	4.15kg (9.13lb)

MODEL	RHEINMETALL MP34(Ö)	MP35 Bgm	VILLAR PEROSA M15
Country of origin	Germany	Germany	Italy
Manufacturer	Swiss Weapons Factory, Solothurn. Steyr Weapons Factory	Junker & Ruh, Karlsruhe	Officine di Villar Perosa
Function	Fully automatic with blowback system	Fully automatic with blowback system	Fully automatic with retarded blowback system
Type of fire	Single-shot or sustained	Single-shot or sustained	Sustained
Overall length	78cm (30.71in)	81cm (32in)	53.3cm (21in)
Barrel length	20cm (7.87in)	18cm (7in)	32cm (12.5in)
Ammunition	9x19mm Parabellum (08 pistol)	9x19mm Parabellum (08 pistol)	9mm Glisenti
Number of riflings	6	6	6
Rifling direction	Right	Right	Right
Muzzle velocity	381m/s (1269ft/s)	c381mps (1269ft/s)	320m/s (1050ft/s)
Rate of fire, cyclic	500 –450rpm	350rpm	1200rpm (per barrel)
Effective range	70m (230ft)	c70m (230ft)	120m (400ft)
Magazine capacity	32 rounds (stick)	20 rounds (stick) or 32 rounds (stick)	25 (per gun)
Sight	Curved sliding sight from 50–500m (55–550 yards)	Curved sliding sight, 50–1000m (55–1100 yards)	Fixed sight
Weight, unloaded	4.05kg (8.91lb)	4.3kg (9.48lb)	6.5kg (14.5lb)

MODEL	THOMPSON MODEL 1921	KONEPISTOOLI (SUOMI) M31	PPD 34/38
Country of origin	USA	Finland	Russia
Manufacturer	Auto Ordnance Corporation	Oy Tikkakoski, Sakara	Various
Function	Fully automatic with retarded blowback system	Fully automatic with blowback system	Fully automatic with blowback system
Type of fire	Sustained	Single-shot or sustained	Single-shot or sustained
Overall length	86cm (33.75in)	87cm (34.25in)	78cm (30.71in)
Barrel length	26.5cm (10.5in)	31.4cm (12.36in)	26.9cm (10.6in)
Ammunition	.45in APC	9x19mm Parabellum (08 pistol)	7.62 Tokarev (P)
Number of riflings	6	6	4
Rifling direction	Right	Right	Right
Muzzle velocity	265m/s (870ft/s)	400m/s (1310ft/s)	488m/s (1600ft/s)
Rate of fire, cyclic	800rpm	900rpm	800rpm
Effective range	120m (400ft)	300m (330 yards)	120m (400ft)
Magazine capacity	30	30 or 50 round box, 71 round drum	25-round box, 71-round drum
Sight	Fixed sight	Fixed sight	Fixed sight
Weight, unloaded	4.87kg (10.75lb)	4.67kg (10.3lb)	3.6kg (8lb)

MODEL	MP38	MP40	LANCHESTER
Country of origin	Germany	Germany	Britain
Manufacturer	ERMA	ERMA	Sterling Armament Company
Function	Fully automatic with blowback system	Fully automatic with blowback system	Fully automatic with blowback system
Type of fire	Automatic only	Automatic only	Single-shot or sustained
Overall length	83cm (32.75in)	83cm (32.75in)	85cm (33.5in)
Barrel length	24.5cm (9.75in)	24.5cm (9.75in)	20.5cm (8in)
Ammunition	9x19mm Parabellum (08 Pistol)	9x19mm Parabellum (08 pistol)	9mm Parabellum
Number of riflings	6	6	6
Rifling direction	Right	Right	Right
Muzzle velocity	381m/s (1269ft/s)	381m/s (1269ft/s)	395m/s (1300ft/s)
Rate of fire, cyclic	500rpm	500rpm	600rpm
Effective range	70m (230ft)	70m (230ft)	70m (230ft)
Magazine capacity	32-round box	32-round box	50-round box
Sight	Fixed sight (100m/110 yards) with flap (200m/220 yards)	Fixed sight (100m/110 yards) with flap (200m/220 yards)	Fixed Rifle No.1 sight
Weight, unloaded	4.1kg (9lb)	3.9kg (8.75lb)	4.35kg (9.5lb)

MODEL	THOMPSON M1A1	STEN Mk II	PPSh41
Country of origin	USA	Britain	Russia
Manufacturer	Auto Ordnance Corporation	Enfield, BSA, Royal Ordnance plus others	Various
Function	Fully automatic with retarded blowback system	Fully automatic with blowback system	Fully automatic with blowback system
Type of fire	Sustained	Single-shot or sustained	Single-shot or sustained
Overall length	81.2cm (32in)	76.2cm (30in)	84cm (33in)
Barrel length	26.5cm (10.5in)	19.5cm (7.75in)	26.5cm (10.5in)
Ammunition	.45in APC	9mm Parabellum	7.62 Tokarev (P)
Number of riflings	6	6	4
Rifling direction	Right	Right	Right
Muzzle velocity	265m/s (870ft/s)	395m/s (1300ft/s)	488m/s (1600ft/s)
Rate of fire, cyclic	600rpm	550rpm	900rpm
Effective range	120m (400ft)	70m (230ft)	120m (400ft)
Magazine capacity	20	32-round box	25-round box, 71-round drum
Sight	Fixed sight	Fixed sight (91m/100yards)	Fixed sight with flap
Weight, unloaded	4.9kg (10.5lb)	2.95kg (6.5lb)	3.6kg (8lb)

MODEL	M3 'Grease Gun'	MODELLO M1938A
Country of origin	USA	Italy
Manufacturer	General Motors and Buffalo Arms Corp	Pietro Beretta SA
Function	Fully automatic with blowback system	Fully automatic with blowback system
Type of fire	Sustained only	Single-shot or sustained
Overall length	74.5cm (29.33in)	95.5cm (37.5in)
Barrel length	20.5cm (8in)	32cm (12.5in)
Ammunition	.45APC	9mm Parabellum
Number of riflings	4	6
Rifling direction	Right	Right
Muzzle velocity	285m/s (870ft/s)	395m/s (1300ft/s)
Rate of fire, cyclic	450rpm	600rpm
Effective range	121m (400ft)	120m (400ft)
Magazine capacity	30-round box	10-, 20-, 30- or 40-round box
Sight	Fixed	Variable (up to 500m/547yards)
Weight, unloaded	3.7kg (8.25lb)	4.2kg (9.25lb)

German Infantry Division World War I

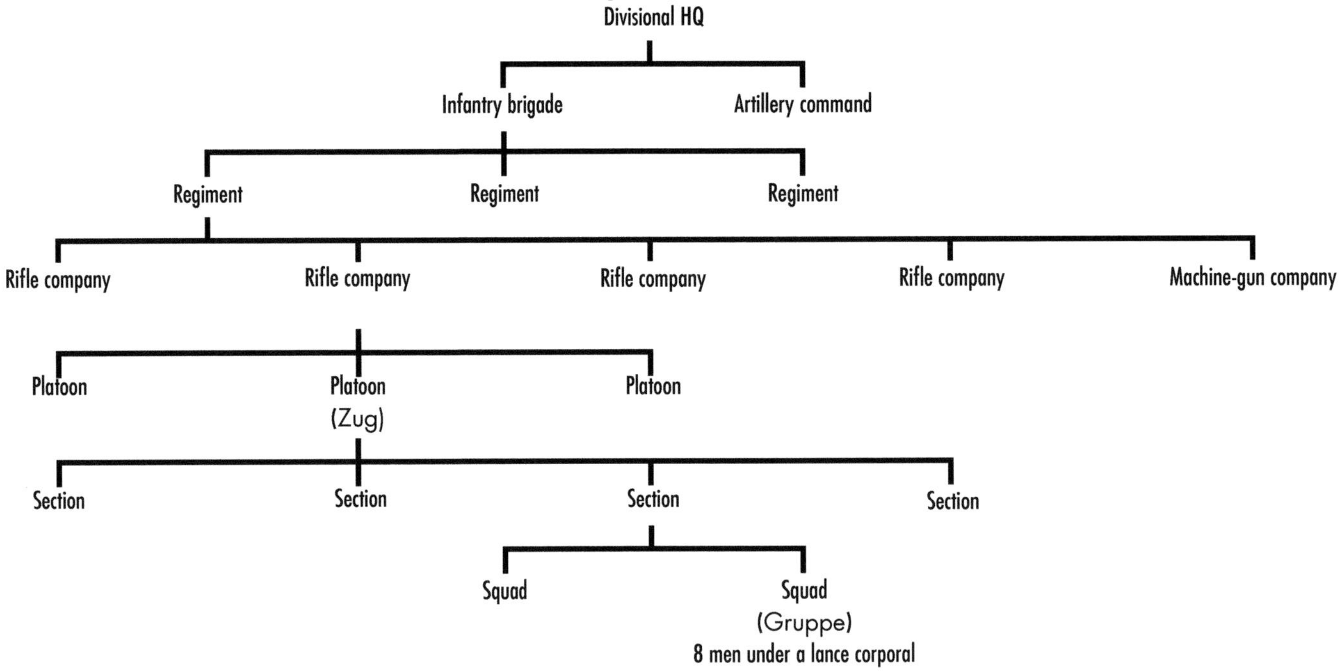

German Infantry Division (1939)

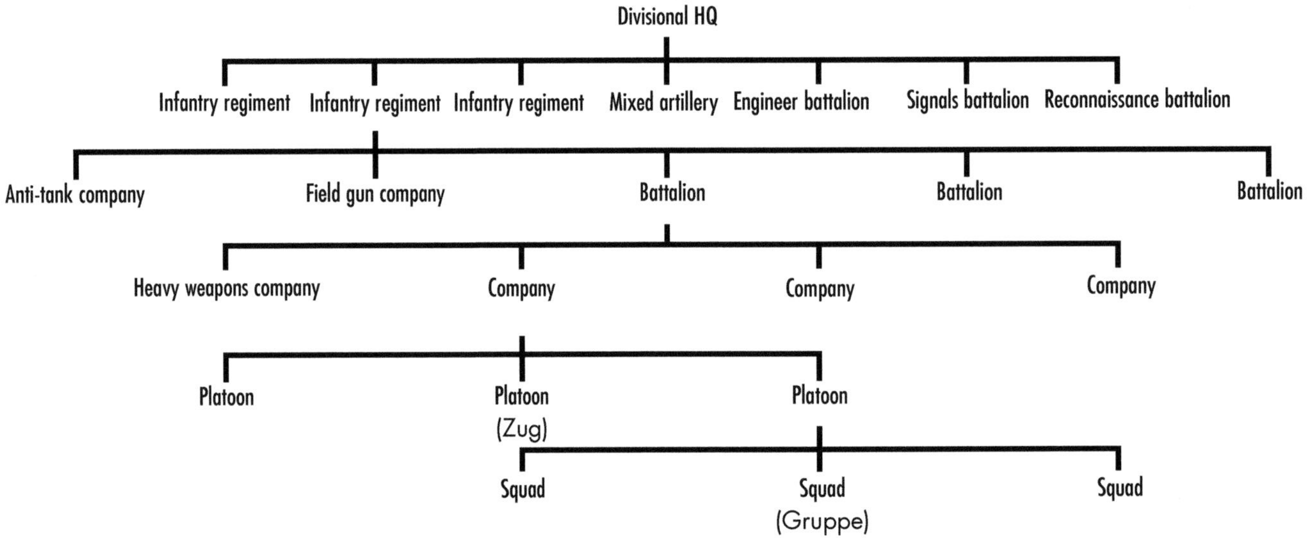

Panzer Grenadier Company
1st November 1944

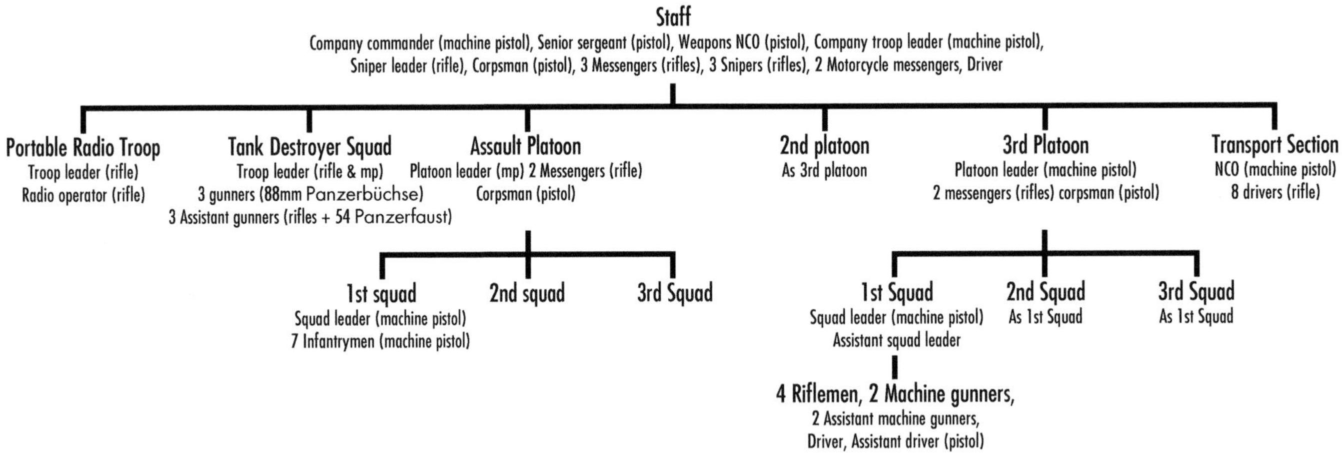

INDEX